THE
OLDER
VOLUNTEER

THE OLDER VOLUNTEER

An Annotated Bibliography

Compiled by

C. Neil Bull
and
Nancy D. Levine

Bibliographies and Indexes in Gerontology, Number 21
Erdman B. Palmore, Series Editor

GREENWOOD PRESS
Westport, Connecticut • London

Library of Congress Cataloging-in-Publication Data

Bull, C. Neil.
   The older volunteer : an annotated bibliography / compiled by C.
Neil Bull and Nancy D. Levine.
      p. cm.—(Bibliographies and indexes in gerontology, ISSN
0743-7560 ; no. 21)
   Includes indexes.
   ISBN 0-313-28125-4 (alk. paper)
   1. Aged volunteers—United States—Bibliography. I. Levine,
Nancy D. II. Title. III. Series.
Z7164.V65B85 1993
[HN90.V64]
016.30526—dc20   92-41898

British Library Cataloguing in Publication Data is available.

Library of Congress Catalog Card Number: 92-41898
ISBN: 0-313-28125-4
ISSN: 0743-7560

First published in 1993

Greenwood Press, 88 Post Road West, Westport, CT 06881
An imprint of Greenwood Publishing Group, Inc.

Printed in the United States of America

10 9 8 7 6 5 4 3 2

Contents

Foreword

The annotated bibliographies in this series provide answers to the fundamental question, "What is known?" Their purpose is simple, yet profound: to provide comprehensive reviews and references for work done in various fields of gerontology. They are based on the fact that it is no longer possible for anyone to comprehend the vast body of research and writing in even one sub-specialty without years of work.

This fact has become true only in recent years. When I was an undergraduate (Class of '52) I think no one at Duke had even heard of gerontology. Almost no one in the world was identified as a gerontologist. Now there are over 6,000 professional members of the Gerontological Society of America. When I was an undergraduate there were no courses in gerontology. Now there are thousands of courses offered by most major (and many minor) colleges and universities. When I was an undergraduate there was only one gerontological journal (the *Journal of Gerontology*, begun in 1945). Now there are over forty professional journals and several dozen books in gerontology published every year.

The reasons for this dramatic growth are well known: the dramatic increase in numbers of aged, the shift from family to public responsibility for the security and care of the elderly, the recognition of aging as a "social problem", and the growth of science in general. It is less well known that this explosive growth in knowledge has developed the need for new solutions to the old problem of comprehending and "keeping up" with a field of knowledge. The old indexes and library card catalogues have become increasingly inadequate for the job. On-line computer indexes and abstracts are one solution but make no evaluative selections nor organize sources logically as is done here. These annotated bibliographies are also more widely available than on-line computer indexes.

These bibliographies will obviously be useful for students and researchers who need to know what research has (or has not) been done in their field. The annotations contain enough information so that the researcher usually does not have to search out the original articles. In the past, the "review of literature" has often been haphazard and was rarely comprehensive, because of the large investment of time (and money) that would be required by a truly comprehensive review. Now, using these bibliographies, researchers can be more confident that they are not missing important previous research; they can be more confident that they are not duplicating past efforts and "reinventing the wheel". It may well become standard and expected practice for researchers to consult such bibliographies, even before they start their research.

The research and writing relevant to the older volunteer has become a large and rapidly growing field. This is attested to by the nearly 400 references in this bibliography and by the wide variety of disciplines represented here. Thus this volume will be useful to professionals and researchers in many different fields.

The authors have done an outstanding job of covering all the recent literature and organizing it into easily accessible form. Not only are the entries organized into seven chapters with seventeen sub-sections, but there is a Preface, an Introduction, an author index, and a subject index. Important entries are cross-referenced between chapters.

Thus, one can look for relevant material in this volume in several ways: (1) look up a given subject in the subject index; (2) look up a given author in the author index; or (3) turn to the chapter/section that covers the topic.

The authors are exceptionally well qualified to prepare this bibliography. Dr. Bull is on the faculty of the Center on Aging Studies at the University of Missouri-Kansas City and has published several articles on related subjects (see the author index). Ms. Levine has just completed her M.A. research and has extensive experience with library data bases.

So it is with great pleasure that we add this bibliography to our series. We believe you will find this volume to be the most useful, comprehensive and easily accessible reference work in its field. I will appreciate any comments you care to send me.

Erdman B. Palmore
Durham, North Carolina

Preface

This bibliography is intended to serve as an up-to-date reference for researchers, practitioners and planners to assist them in their future work on the older volunteer. In completing this bibliography, we were not initially aware of how widespread the numerous sources were. It soon became imperative that we limit the work to a very specific set of literature. In order to put a boundary around the subject matter we first had to decide upon eligibility requirements for inclusion.

To be included, a work had to focus on the older volunteer rather than consist of general literature on volunteers who may or may not deal with older people. With such a focus in mind, we wish to alert the reader that we consciously excluded certain related subject areas. We now wish to outline these restrictions. First, at the most general level, we have excluded most of the area of "altruism," which covers not only the giving of time or help, but also money in the form of philanthropy and charity. Second, we have excluded the literature on voluntary organization participants because the volunteer component of such participation is very difficult to measure. Third, we have omitted much of the literature on visiting, friendship and neighboring even though there can be and often is some voluntary help taking place in these interactions. Fourth, we have excluded from the vast literature on inter-generational relations, those programs which have focused on the young helping the elderly and included only those materials pertinent to the elderly, as volunteers, helping the young. Finally, we have not included materials that cover countries other than countries located in North America unless publication occurred in an American Journal.

With these limits in mind, we completed a search for all materials covered by our subject and for the period from 1980 to 1991. A large number of potential sources of information was used, including previous bibliographies, some of which are referenced in this book. The usual computer searches were completed, as well as looking through the proceedings of national meetings for paper presentations. A wide range of terms were used to ensure that the concepts of both elderly and volunteer were covered. In all, over 700 individual citations were found ranging all the way from books, book chapters, articles and paper presentations, to reports and theses and dissertations. Some of these materials were impossible to find due to the holding libraries' non-lending policies or because the materials were out of print. Such citations were dropped unless the materials were judged to be available at cost, in which case, they were simply referenced but not annotated.

We have organized the annotations into seven major chapters, and where applicable, due to the multiplicity of topics covered, included an annotated work in one chapter, but merely referenced it in another.

The bibliography begins with materials which examine the general picture of older volunteers but contain little, if any, original empirical data. The following two chapters focus more specifically on research findings with Chapter 2 covering the presentation, either as primary or secondary data, of studies based upon national samples, and Chapter 3 contains empirical findings with a focus on four major topics: social and psychological characteristics of older volunteers, motivations, barriers, and the impact of volunteering on older people and/or the older volunteer.

Chapter 4 is devoted to specific settings in which older volunteers are utilized, including educational institutions, health care institutions, and religious institutions. Literature pertaining predominately to national programs--RSVP, Foster Grandparent Program, the Peace Corps, and roles for retired professionals, may be found in Chapter 5.

Chapter 6 includes materials which focus upon the evaluation or review of specific models or programs, and the final chapter (Chapter 7) contains materials pertinent to special populations: widows and widowers, developmentally disabled/visually impaired, racial or ethnic minorities, rural populations, and older volunteers in law enforcement or as aides to crime victims.

C. Neil Bull
Nancy D. Levine

Kansas City, Missouri

Acknowledgments

We would like to acknowledge and express our sincere gratitude to the many individuals, from numerous corners of the country, who assisted us in locating the original 700 plus references.

In particular, we would like to thank the following individuals for their invaluable assistance and/or advice: the reference and interlibrary loan staff at the Miller Nichols Library, University of Missouri-Kansas City; Share DeCroix Bane and Sandra Leigh Custard of the National Resource Center for Rural Elderly; Drs. Susan Maizel Chambré and Lucy Rose Fischer, whose works are included in the bibliography, and finally, a special thanks to Pat Cundiff, of Heart of America United Way-Volunteer Center.

We must also recognize the many authors, whose works we have reviewed, for their contribution to our understanding of the older volunteer.

Introduction

There is a growing recognition that, in our society, the role of the volunteer, especially the older volunteer, will continue to expand and become essential to the provision of many social services that cannot be met either by the state or the private sector. The utilization of older volunteers enables federal, state, local, and private funding for programs to be stretched at a time when these resources are becoming less available.

There appear to be several factors driving the movement toward the increased use of older volunteers. First, and most important, is the sheer number of elderly, which is projected to double from 31.5 million in 1990 to approximately 65.6 million by the year 2030. Added to this pressure is the faster rate of increase among the frail elderly, with the "over 85" population growing from 10 percent of the total number of elderly in 1990 to more than 15 percent by the year 2000.

The second factor, alluded to above, is that government monies available for the provision of services are continually under strain, due to overspending and increased competition for these scarce resources.

Third, there has been a growing shortage of traditional volunteers-- middle-aged females. As ever-increasing numbers of females participate full-time in the work force, they can no longer afford the time or loss of wages in order to begin or continue in their volunteer roles.

A fourth factor pertains to the increasing numbers of individuals who are retiring, either early or on time, with many years of active life remaining, thus producing a potential pool from which to draw.

Fifth, reluctance to use the elderly as volunteers has diminished as the stereotypes of the older volunteer have been debunked. There is now enough empirical evidence which indicates that the older volunteer is trainable, reliable, and when asked, wishes to contribute to society. In addition, older volunteers have been successfully utilized as role models who motivate other potential older volunteers. It is difficult for a 65 year old to use his or her age as an avoidance or incompetence rationale when asked by an 80 year old, who has possibly performed the same activity for 15 years.

Finally, the major government agencies have recognized the importance of this third sector--the volunteer and voluntary organizations--which can go a long way to help with community services. Where there are acute shortages of services, as within inner-cities or isolated rural areas, the recruitment, training and retention of older volunteers becomes crucial. These service shortages dictate that the resources intended to meet the needs of the elderly be used in the most innovative, appropriate and efficient manner. Duplication of effort, ignorance of effective programming and poor resource allocation strategies are simply not acceptable. The use of volunteers, especially those knowledgeable about their local community, is a key component of any service delivery system and when wisely employed, is highly beneficial both for the volunteer and the recipient.

The relationship between volunteering and aging represents an emerging role in our society--a role of interdependence that both counters the view of older persons as dependent and powerless and supports the idea of older persons who desire authority and independence. Volunteering, therefore, contains numerous benefits, not only for the recipients, but for the volunteers as well.

A review of the materials in this bibliography, it is hoped, will be helpful to researchers, service providers, as well as the older volunteer in providing the background necessary to increase the interdependency between the elderly at the person-to-person level, between organizations, and between older persons and organizations.

Chapter 1
General

1. Aucoin, James. (1984, June-July). Volunteers for the environment. Modern Maturity, 27(3), 24-27.

   The author writes to show the elderly how they can volunteer in the many growing not-for-profit organizations that are dealing with environmental issues. A list of eight such organizations is given, as well as a short description of each.

2. Baines, Elizabeth Murrow. (1986). Volunteerism and the older adult as benefactor and beneficiary: A selected review of the literature. Working Paper Series, The Strom Thurmond Institute, (Serial No. WP103086).

   This useful review article focuses on the major characteristics of the older volunteer, the major programs, the benefits and consequences of being a volunteer and the major problems associated with the volunteer role. Implications for future research and policy are outlined together with a set of fifteen recommendations.

3. Baines, Elizabeth Murrow. (1986). Volunteerism and aging: A bibliography. Working Paper Series. Clemson, SC: Clemson University, Strom Thurmond Institute of Government and Public Affairs. (ERIC Document Reproduction Service No. ED 313 542)

This is a very useful bibliography of 264 works with some annotations, divided into the following subject matters: motivation, programs and case studies, and general works dealing with elderly volunteers. Included is a section on volunteers working with elderly institutionalized and non-institutionalized elderly clinents, and a section on general references as well.

4.   Biegel, David E., Shore, Barbara K., & Gordon, Elizabeth. (1984). Building support networks for the elderly: Theory and applications. Beverly Hills, CA: Sage.

As part of the support network for the elderly, the authors cover several topics that are of interest: the link to volunteers as helpers, the ideas surrounding the topic of mutual aid and self help, and the use of neighbors as resources. The theories about social networks and the frameworks surrounding intervention strategies are very useful.

5.   Biegel, David E., & Napersteck, Arthur J. (Eds.). (1982). Community support systems and mental health: Practice, policy and research. New York: Springer.

This edited book has two chapters that are of interest: Chapter 9 examines at the roles for informal helpers in the delivery of human services including the role of the volunteer. Chapter 11 looks at the role of senior centers as part of the support network and includes discussion of the roles of volunteers and voluntary organizations.

6.   Brodsky, Ruthan. (1987, April-May). As much to gain as give. Modern Maturity, 29(2), 46-50.

Using examples of the many programs and roles that are available to the older volunteer, this article is used to show that retirement, work and volunteering are not mutually exclusive and that life satisfaction comes from many roles.

7.   Bull, C. Neil, & Payne, Barbara. (1988). Brief bibliography: A selective annotated bibliography for gerontology instruction. Washington, DC: Association for Gerontology in Higher Education.

This is a short bibliography of 25 entries to be used by educators wishing to quickly look at the better materials that can be used in the classroom setting. Covered are the areas of: theoretical models, concepts of volunteerism, demographic statistics, bibliographies, programs and guides, as well as works that look at volunteers in specific settings, such as churches, education, hospitals, home-care and the neighborhood/community.

8.   Chambré, Susan M., & Lowe, Ida B. (1983-84, Winter). Volunteering and the aged: A bibliography for researchers and practitioners. The Journal of Volunteer Administration, 2(2), 35-43.

To date this is one of the better bibliographies dealing with the older volunteer. Although not annotated, the 155 references are split into the following main categories: general, administrative issues, barriers, empirical studies, social characteristics associated with volunteering, motivations, impact of volunteering, programs, volunteer settings and legislation and advocacy.

9.   Cnaan, Ram A., & Cwikel, Julie G. (1991). Elderly volunteers: Assessing their potential as an untapped resource. Manuscript submitted for publication.

Many policy analysts and researchers consider the elderly to be an untapped source for volunteer recruitment and this paper identifies the origins of this societal expectation and its actualization. Presented, in addition, are analyses of factors contributing to and deterring the actual deployment of large numbers of elderly as volunteers.

10.   Cnaan, Ram A., & Goldberg-Glen, Robin S. (1989, November). Testing theories of adaptation to old age through volunteer traits, management, activities, and satisfaction. The Gerontologist, 29, 123A. Abstract of paper presented at the 42nd annual meeting of the Gerontological Society of America, Minneapolis, MN.

To test several social theories of adaptation to old age, this paper examines the traits, management, activities, and satisfaction of 131 elderly volunteers and 121 young volunteers with, where applicable, 135 non-volunteers. The major findings support continuity theory as it relates to volunteer participation throughout the life cycle.

11.   Committee on an Aging Society. (1986). Productive roles in an older society. Washington, DC: National Academy Press.

This excellent volume is the product of a symposium held to look at the general topic of unpaid productive roles. The symposium committee starts the volume with a report summarizing their recommendations, and the discussions on which they were based, followed by a presentation of the papers commissioned for the symposium on the topics of:

the economics of volunteerism, the older volunteer resource, unpaid productive activity over the life course and socioeconomic aspects of future unpaid productive roles.

12.   Community action stirs senior potential. (1980, May-Jun). Aging, 307-308, 10-11.

The use, number and types of programs which utilized older volunteers are reviewed in this brief, general article.

13.   Daniels, Arlene Kaplan. (1985, April). Good times and good works: The place of sociability in the work of women volunteers. Social Problems, 32, 363-374.

This is one of the few studies that examines the volunteer activities of elite women in their pursuit of sociability work--the promotion of charitable causes. The study highlights the clash between expressive versus instrumental work in that it is problematic how to reward and recognize the social value of this "invisible" work.

14.   Department of Corporate Planning and Evaluation National Headquarters, American Red Cross. (1988). Volunteer 2000 study volume I: Findings and recommendations. Washington, DC: The American National Red Cross.

This publication by the American Red Cross reports the findings of a study intended to provide a current, organization-wide data base on volunteers. While primarily addressing issues in volunteerism and volunteer administration within the Red Cross, section IV presents nationally projected trends and conditions (e.g., the aging population) having relevance to volunteerism in general. In addition, demographics on age distribution of the volunteer force within the Red Cross are presented.

15.   Dychtwald, Ken, & Flower, Joe. (1989). Age wave: The challenges and opportunities of an aging America. Los Angeles: Jeremy P. Tarcher.

As part of this general work, which examined the implications for society with regard to the ever increasing number of elderly, is a chapter titled "Wisdom in Action." This chapter takes a quick look at two roles other than the leisure role: those of education and volunteerism. Attention is paid to different types of volunteer roles with a special section on corporate-sponsored volunteer corps.

16.   Ellis, Susan J., & Noyes, Katherine H. (1990). <u>By the people: A</u>
        <u>history of Americans as volunteers</u>. San Francisco: Jossey Bass.

        This book lacks much material on the older volunteer until the very
        end. However, the historical roots of volunteerism in the United States
        is very well presented and useful to the understanding of the role of
        volunteer activities in our society.

17.   Fischer, Lucy Rose, Mueller, Daniel P., & Cooper, Phillip W. (1991).
        Older volunteers: A discussion of the Minnesota Senior Study. <u>The</u>
        <u>Gerontologist</u>, <u>31</u>, 183-194.

        A new conceptual model is presented for classifying volunteer roles
        based on the three dimensions of whether volunteer service is "formal"
        or "informal," a regular or occasional time commitment, and the nature
        of the service activity (person-to-community, person-to-object, or
        person-to-person). The purpose of the new classification is to try to
        overcome some of the problems of definition and classification that
        have confounded previous analyses.

18.   Fischer, Lucy Rose, & Schaffer, Kay. (1992). <u>Time and Talent:</u>
        <u>Recruiting and working with older volunteers</u>. Manuscript submitted
        for publication.

        Intended primarily as a means of making research accessible to
        practitioners who work with older volunteers, this book offers 1) a
        synthesis of research relevant to volunteering--especially volunteering
        among the elderly, and 2) practical information pertinent to recruiting,
        retaining and working with older volunteers.

19.   Fleisher, Dorothy, & Kaplan, Barbara Hade. (1984, November). A
        policy imperative: Structuring volunteer roles to encourage long-term
        commitments from older people. <u>The Gerontologist</u>, <u>24</u>, 295.

        With the use of data from 200 older volunteers, the authors outline
        their findings which show that the following variables contributed to
        satisfaction and commitment: continuity with past work role, career
        ladder opportunities, and prestige status of the role within the agency.
        In addition, for those in policy making roles in the sixteen health, edu-
        cation, and social service agencies, active participation was correlated
        with opportunities for involvement in budgeting, reviewing of grants,
        investigating complaints, reimbursement for expenses, and instrumental
        and expressive benefits received.

20.   Garbascz, Christopher, & Thayer, Mark A. (1983). An experiment in valuing companion services. The Journal of Human Resources, 18(1), 147-152.

This short article is one of a few that deals with the determination of the value in cost/benefit terms of a Senior Companion Program. The data show that if the programs were cut by either 25 or 75 percent, such a reduction would not be justified on the basis of cost/benefit analysis.

21.   Hanna, William. (1981, Summer). Senior advocacy: Diverse, successful and evolving. Generations, 5(4), 20-21, 48.

This short article looks at the volunteer role of the elderly in the area of advocacy and outlines examples of the process used with a focus on: The Senior Lobby, The Silver Haired Legislature, national organizations, and political parties.

22.   Harman, John D. (Ed.). (1982). Volunteerism in the eighties: Fundamental issues in voluntary action. Washington, DC: University Press of America.

This collection of eighteen essays covers a full range of topics covering volunteerism in general. Part 1 looks at some of the conceptual issues that have emerged in the 70's. The second section looks at the conflict within the volunteer sector between professionalization and the reliance on volunteers. The third section looks at volunteerism in a democracy.

23.   Havir, Linda. (1986, July-Sept). An evaluation of older volunteers as telephone interviewers. Journal of Voluntary Action Research, 15(3), 45-53.

This article looks at the use of 67 older volunteers who were used as telephone interviewers in a needs assessment survey of a large, randomly selected sample of older adults. The results showed a cooperation rate of 81 percent. The recruitment, training and problems encountered are outlined as well.

24.   Height, Dorothy I., Toya, James, Kamikawa, Louise, & Maldonado, David. (1981, Summer). Senior volunteering in minority communities. Generations, 5(4), 14-17, 46.

This brief, but very useful, article examines the roles played by elderly minority volunteers in their communities. The authors, looking at

Blacks, Native Americans, Hispanics and Pacific/Asians show how the term "volunteer" must be carefully applied in each community to capture the depth of activities and roles played by the elderly.

25.   Herzog, A. Regula, & House, James S. (1991, Winter). Productive activities and aging well. Generations, 15(1), 49-54.

In this article, the author looks at the concept of productivity as it relates to aging successfully. Several sets of data are presented in which volunteer work is seen as the activity most beneficial to the volunteer, and second most beneficial to others. The data also supports the notion that older people feel they should contribute through service, to the well-being of others.

26.   Hutton, William R. (1981). Volunteering: Unaffordable luxury for the elderly. Generations, 5(4), 12-13, 47.

This article looks at the tension that is occurring between the use of older volunteers to do work while at the same time many low-income elderly could use a part-time job. The author is opposed to any programs that exploit older volunteers when others could receive a nominal wage.

27.   Jones, Sidney. (1986, September). The elders: A new generation. Ageing and Society, 6(3), 313-331.

This article looks at the growing health, wealth and satisfaction of the elderly and offers examples of key areas of personal experience and social life. Attention is focused on education, leisure retirement, voluntary activity, and other personal attributes.

28.   Kahn, E. (1986). A legend in her own town. 50 Plus, 26(7), 34-37.

This essay is a case study of an older female volunteer who, both by mail and phone, and through personal visits, is a companion and helper in her community of New London, New Hampshire.

29.   Keller, John. (Ed.). (1981, Summer). Elders and volunteerism (Special issue). Generations, 5(4).

This highly recommended special issue of Generations contains nineteen articles which address a diversity of issues related to senior volunteerism and would serve as an excellent source for the novice in the field.

30.   Kosberg, Jordan, & Garcia, Juanita. (1985). Issues in assessing community resources for the leisure-time needs of the elderly. Journal of Sociology and Social Welfare, 12(4), 777-797.

        In this general article about the growth in leisure following retirement, the authors outline and describe in detail, some of the activities that may be used to overcome the potential problem of boredom. Described are: leisure resources, recreation, education, volunteerism, voluntary association participation, familialism, and sold-itarity activities.

31.   Kouri, Mary K. (1984). From retirement to re-engagement. The Futurist, 18(3), 35-42.

        This is a general article looking at the rejection of the traditional retirement lifestyle of full-time leisure and outlining how seniors have re-engaged. The topics covered are: education, work, mentoring, and community service.

32.   Kouri, Mary K. (1990). Volunteerism and older adults. Santa Barbara, CA: ABC-CLIO.

        This is an excellent book for both the elderly seeking volunteer opportunities and service providers using volunteers. There are two major parts: Part 1 deals with the history of volunteerism, finding volunteer opportunities and contains suggestions for volunteer directors. Part 2 provides a very extensive resource guide, giving directories of organizations, government agencies, and self-help groups, followed by an annotated bibliography of printed materials and a separate annotated directory of non-printed materials.

33.   Lackner, Robin, & Koeck, Cynthia. (1980, December). The elderly as Resource: An examination of volunteerism among the elderly in Minnesota. St. Paul: Minnesota State Planning Agency, Human Resources Planning.

        This technical report describes the various activities in which elderly volunteers engage with emphasis on: 1) the types of groups involved in volunteerism, and 2) the effect of volunteering on the older volunteer, agencies, clients, and the government. The major issues surrounding volunteerism and the impact of the changing populations on volunteer behavior are discussed.

34.   Loughlin, Terence. (1981, Summer). Older volunteers: A share of the action and power. Generations, 5(4), 22-23.

The author of this article demonstrates, with illustrations, how effective older volunteers can be as members on advisory boards in both government and non-profit service organizations.

35.   Midlarsky, Elizabeth, & Kahana, Eva. (1984). Helping by the elderly: A study of its nature, antecedents and outcomes (Final Report). Washington, DC: AARP Andrus Foundation.

The focus of this research is on helping behaviors by the elderly living in senior citizens' housing sites. As an excellent final report, in which the theory used and the methods employed to collect the data are very well outlined, this document shows how the theory of altruism can be generalized to cover helping behaviors by the elderly.

36.   Monk, Abraham. (1987). Volunteers. In George Maddox, et al. (Eds.). Encyclopedia on aging (pp. 685-687). New York: Springer.

A short history of the research on the older volunteer starts this entry and is followed by a review of the characteristics of those who do volunteer. Several new national programs are reviewed and the relationship between volunteering and life satisfaction is discussed.

37.   O'Connell, Brian, & O'Connell, Ann Brown. (1989). Volunteers in action. Washington, DC: The Foundation Center.

This is an excellent book which shows the breadth of the types of volunteer work that is being carried out in America. With the use of many descriptions of volunteer programs, including some using older volunteers, this publication looks not only at programs in action, but how to become part of that action. The future of volunteerism is discussed with a focus on the younger volunteer.

38.   Payne, Barbara. (1983). Volunteerism and transportation of the elderly and handicapped. Specialized Transportation: Planning and Practice, 14(3), 28-34.

This article is a general introduction used to push for the use of volunteers in specialized transportation for the elderly and handicapped. Covered are the topics of changes in the role of the older volunteer, what is known about why the elderly volunteer, a review of how they are used, and a brief overview of the issues of liability, cost effectiveness, pay, and financial support.

39.   Payne, Barbara, & Bull, C. Neil. (1982, August). <u>Voluntary associa-
        tions and volunteerism in a community context: A theoretical model</u>.
        Paper presented at the International Sociological Association, 10th
        World Congress, Mexico City, Mexico.

        This paper outlines a holistic model, adapted from Warren's community
        theory and Payne's volunteer role restructuring model, to be used in the
        interpretation of research on both voluntary association participation
        and volunteering in a community context. Data from a ten year
        longitudinal study of older volunteers are used to illustrate the model.

40.   Payne, Barbara, & Bull, C. Neil. (1985). The older volunteer: The
        case for interdependence. In W. A. Peterson & J. Quadagno (Eds.).
        <u>Social bonds in later life</u> (pp. 251-272). Beverly Hills, CA: Sage.

        That the volunteer role represents an emerging form of interdependence
        is illustrated with historical data and the longitudinal study in the 1970's
        of a panel of volunteers in Shepherd Centers in Kansas City and
        Atlanta. A community model of voluntary organization is outlined
        showing the move toward relying on peer interdependency to meet
        normal aging needs and social meaning.

41.   Pepper, Claude. (1981, Summer). Senior volunteerism: Alive and well
        in the '80's. <u>Generations</u>, <u>5</u>(4), 6-7.

        In this short, general article, a review is made of government programs
        that have been set up to help older volunteers. The question of
        reimbursement for volunteer work is examined at, as well as how
        partnerships are being formed between the private and public sectors.

42.   Rakocy, Genevieve. (1981). Senior volunteers: Finding and Keeping
        them. <u>Generations</u>, <u>5</u>(4), 36-37, 45.

        This article reviews the growing competition for older volunteers.
        Recruitment and turnover are examined with special emphasis on
        training, and demonstrating to volunteers, the value of their work and
        the fact that they can be liberated from the ageism stereotypes.

43.   Romero, Carol Jusenius. (1987). Retirement and older Americans'
        participation in volunteer activities. In Steven H. Sandell (Ed.), <u>The
        Problem isn't age: Work and older Americans</u> (pp. 218-227). New
        York: Praeger.

This chapter, as part of a larger volume on work and retirement, is a very short review of the extent of volunteerism, and represents a conceptual framework to explain why people volunteer. Empirical evidence to support such a framework is provided.

44.   Salman, Robert. (1985). The use of aged volunteers: Individual and organizational considerations. In George S. Getzel, & Joanna M. Mellor (Eds.), Gerontological social work practice in the community (pp. 211-223). New York: Haworth.

A short review chapter of the history of the issues which set up the myths surrounding the non-use of older volunteers is followed by a discussion of how the role of the agency can change such attitudes. Using characteristics of volunteer staff, the author suggests ways in which they can best be used in an agency.

45.   Schwartz, Florence S. (Ed.). (1984). Voluntarism and social work practice: A growing collaboration. New York: University Press of America.

This collection of essays looks at the relationship between the role of volunteers and their use in social agencies. Although the works cover volunteers of all ages--with a heavy emphasis on social work--one chapter, by Seguin (see entry # 336) looks specifically at senior adult volunteers.

46.   Seguin, Mary M., & McConney, Polly F. (1985, Spring). Team building and older volunteers. The Journal of Volunteer Administration, 3(3), 39-46.

47.   Smith, David Horton, MacCaulay, Jacqueline & Associates. (1980). Participation in social and political activities. San Fancisco: Jossey-Bass.

Although this edited book does not specifically deal with the elderly, it is included in this bibliography as one of the better collections of articles that deal with the general subject of voluntary participation and in several chapters, age as a variable is included. Attention should be given to the chapter by Payne on nonassociational religious participation.

48.   Stowell, Anita M. (1981, Summer). NRTA-AARP volunteers: For the benefit of all. Generations, 5(4), 38-39.

In this short article, the author reviews the legislative and program
initiatives of the American Association of Retired Persons' National
Legislative Councils. More than 40,000 volunteers are involved in
either the legislative or community service programs.

49.   Taylor, Susan Champlin. (1990, April-May). Talents, tools and time.
       Modern Maturity, 79-84.

       This is a short essay on the general subject of the older volunteer
       showing who volunteers (1988 data), how to get people involved, and
       outlining for the individual, who and where to make contact in order
       to learn more about volunteer opportunities in their community.

50.   Turner, Howard B. (in press). Older volunteers: An assessment of two
       theories. Educational Gerontology.

       As a test of activity versus exchange theory, this paper outlines a train-
       the-trainer model using forty-one older volunteers who received 28
       hours of classroom training and then were expected to conduct in-
       service training for social service personnel. The longitudinal data
       showed limited and inconsistent support for either theory and the author
       suggests the use of the continuity perspective to explain the results.

51.   U.S. Congress, Senate. (1988). Older American volunteer programs.
       Washington, DC: U.S. Government Printing Office.

52.   Van til, Jon. (1988). Mapping the third sector: Voluntarism in a
       changing social economy. New York: The Foundation Center.

       We include this book in the bibliography, even though there is little
       specific reference to older volunteers, because of its importance in
       painting a broad picture of the field of volunteerism. There are over
       thirty pages of references, making this work an excellent starting point
       for those unfamiliar with the area of voluntary action.

53.   Wilson, Marlene. (1990). You can make a difference: Helping others
       and yourself through volunteering. Boulder, CO: Volunteer Manage-
       ment Associates.

       This informative book, intended primarily for potential volunteers,
       includes much information pertinent to the elderly volunteer. Chapter
       7, "Sharing Your Lifetime Experience," is especially significant for
       this group and includes brief case histories in addition to a partial

list/descriptions of senior volunteer groups. Volunteer organizations for seniors are listed and described in Appendix B, whereas Appendix A contains a list of volunteer centers in the United States and Canada.

54.   Worthy, Edmund H., Eisman, Carol, & Wood, Rene. (1982). Voluntary action and older people: An annotated bibliography. Washington DC: National Council on the Aging.

This 1982 annotated bibliography of nearly 100 items is divided into two main parts with the first five sections focusing on self-help/mutual aid and the second half dealing with older volunteers under the four section headings of: Overview and Issues, Statistics and Data Bases, Research Perspectives, and Programmatic Implications.

Chapter 2
Statistics and National Databases

55.   Chambré, Susan Maizel. (1985). <u>Correlates of volunteer participation by the elderly: Final report to the AARP Andrus Foundation</u>. New York: City University of New York, Bernard M. Baruch College.

Using the 1981 data from the Harris national survey of people over 60 (N=2,090) this study examines the major correlates of volunteer participation and finds that strongest influence is, in order: general activity level, education, age, and life satisfaction. Recommendations for recruitment and retention are made based on the findings.

56.   Chambré, Susan M. (1987). <u>Good deeds in old age: Volunteering by the new leisure class</u>. Lexington, MA: Lexington Books.

This book contains a secondary analysis of data from a national survey sponsored by the National Council on Aging and conducted by Louis Harris and Associates. It focuses on six aspects of volunteering by the elderly: social characteristics of volunteers, substitute for role loss in old age, contribution to higher life satisfaction, factors which influence volunteer participation, and implications for designing and administering volunteer programs.

57.   Chambré, Susan M. (1991).   Volunteerism in an aging society.
        Working Papers Series, Center for the Study of Philanthropy.   New
        York: City University of New York, Graduate School and University
        Center.

        This is an excellent review paper of the trends in older volunteerism
        using data collected in national studies from 1965 to 1989. The author
        shows the increase in participation in volunteer work and then reviews
        some of the possible causes for this change, looking at the characteris-
        tics of volunteers, changes in social policy, role loss substitution,
        fictive kinship roles, work substitution, and future trends.

58.   Chambré, Susan M. (in press). Volunteering by Elders: Demographic
        and policy trends, past and future. In Resourceful aging: Today and
        tomorrow, conference proceedings.   Washington, DC: American
        Association of Retired Persons.

59.   De Combray, Natalie. (1987). Volunteering in America. American
        Demographics, 9(3), 50-52.

        Many of the statistics used to describe 1) volunteer demographics
        (including age), and 2) the budgets of voluntary organizations, are
        reviewed in this essay.

60.   Ferris, James M. (1988, March). The use of volunteers in public
        service production: Some demand and supply considerations. Social
        Science Quarterly, 69(1), 3-23.

        In this article, local government reliance on the use of volunteers in
        public service production is examined with regard to supply and
        demand factors.   Based upon analyses of a national cross-sectional
        sample, findings indicate that there is greater use of volunteers if the
        jurisdiction; 1) has a high tax burden, 2) operates under a manager
        government form, 3) has a relatively large population 4) is poor, and
        5) is not constrained by tax limitation.

61.   Gallup Organization, Inc. (1981).   Americans volunteer - 1981.
        Princeton, NJ: Author.

        This volume is a description of the national probability sample of 1601
        adults and 152 teenagers carried out by the Gallup Organization in 1981
        to determine: the number of people who volunteer, the type of
        volunteer work, the amount of time devoted to volunteer work, changes
        in amount and type, and the reasons given for volunteering or not

volunteering. A technical appendix gives the survey instrument used and the sampling tolerances.

62.   Herzog, A. Regula, Kahn, Robert L., Morgan, James N., Jackson, James S., & Antounucci, Toni C. (1989). Age differences in productive activities. The Journal of Gerontology, 44(4), S129-S138.

The data from a national household survey of 3,617 adults, aged 25 and older, was collected in 1986 in order to examine age differences in both paid and unpaid work. Using the older respondents, this article shows that the elderly participate in many unpaid activities at levels that are comparable to both the middle-aged and younger populations. The activities included: volunteer work in organizations, informal help with others, rearing of children, and repair and maintenance of the home.

63.   Hodgkinson, Virginia A., & Weitzman, Murray S. (1988). Giving and volunteering in the United States. Washington, DC: Independent Sector.

This is the first of a biennial series of surveys on giving and volunteering in the United States, in which 2,775 adults were interviewed in the spring of 1988. Age is included as a variable and major questions on volunteering behavior, as well as motives for giving and volunteering, are addressed. General questions about the role of charitable organizations, the individual and government in providing help to others are likewise included. This is an excellent data set--quite useful in the acquisition of a general understanding of volunteering.

64.   Hodgkinson, Virginia A., & Weitzman, Murray S. (Eds.). (1989). Dimensions of the Independent Sector: A statistical profile (3rd ed.). Washington, DC: Independent Sector.

This report, based upon various sources both public and private, is the third such report in a biennial series of statistical profiles on the independent (voluntary) sector in the United States. Contained within are data on age of volunteers, as well as trends in volunteering.

65.   Hodgkinson, Virginia A., & Weitzman, Murray S. (1990). Giving and volunteering in the United States: Findings from a national survey. Washington, DC: Independent Sector.

While devoted to volunteering in general, this publication contains a wealth of demographic information on this national sample, among which "age" is one variable. The work covers the second biennial survey done by the Independent Sector, using a sample of 2,727 adults interviewed in their homes in the spring of 1990. This is a very useful national data set.

66.   Hulbert, James R., & Chase, Richard A. (1991, May). Retiree volunteers and the agencies they serve: A national survey (RRF Grant No. 90-81). St. Paul, MN: Amherst H. Wilder Foundation, Wilder Research Center.

This research is based on data collected from 560 corporate retirees and 71 non-profit agencies who were contacted in order to yield a representative picture of the lives of retiree volunteers and volunteering. Volunteers in the sample account for three in five of the retirees. Data presented concerns 1) the characteristics of the volunteers in general, 2) attitudes toward volunteering by both volunteers and non-volunteers, and 3) comparisons between volunteers and non-volunteers on several demographic and outcome variables.

67.   Juster, F. Thomas, & Stafford, Frank P. (Eds.). (1985). Time, goods, and well-being. Ann Arbor: University of Michigan, Survey Research Center, Institute for Social Research.

The purpose of this book is to provide an overview of the typical patterns of time use of American adults in the mid-1970's. Embedded in the many tables are the time spent in volunteering or helping organizations--a useful reference piece but not directly focusing on older volunteers.

68.   Louis Harris and Associates. (1981, November). Aging in the eighties: America in transition. Washington, DC: National Council on the Aging.

As part of this national study carried out by Louis Harris and Associates for the National Council on Aging, interviewing 3,327 people of which 1,837 were over the age of 65, a very important data set is presented on volunteerism. Good data are presented on: activities at which "a lot of time" is spent, attendance at senior citizen clubs, and more importantly, volunteerism among the public over age 65 as well as numbers of potential volunteers.

69.   McClelland, Kent A. (1982). Self-conception and life satisfaction: Integrating aged subculture and Activity Theory. Journal of Gerontology, 37, 723-732.

The major thrust of this article is the relationship between self-conception and life-satisfaction. Using the 1975 national Harris study, one of the control measures was the degree of social activity. "Doing volunteer work" was one of four components of this variable. Self-conception was found to be an important intervening variable between social activity and life-satisfaction.

70.   McLaughlin, Frank. (1983). Volunteerism and life satisfaction in older people. The Gerontologist, 23, 69. Abstract of paper presented at the 36th annual meeting of the Gerontological Society of America.

With the use of a subsample from the 1975 Harris survey, this paper tests activity theory to which is added the concept of salience--the importance of the activity to the individual. The data, using multiple classification analysis, shows that volunteering has no significant association with life satisfaction in this representative sample of older people.

71.   Marriott Senior Living Services and United States Administration on Aging. (1991, April). Marriott Seniors volunteerism Study. Washington, DC: Marriott Senior Living Services.

This is an excellent summary of the national 1991 study of 962 elderly (60 years and older) which examines many variables associated with volunteering. The data include: estimates of who performed volunteer work, the potential volunteers, hours and days volunteering occurred, reasons for volunteering, the demographics of the volunteers, the places (organizations) in which volunteering occurred, and the order of preference concerning who volunteers liked to work with.

72.   Schiman, Cathy, & Lordeman, Ann. (1989, December). A study of the use of volunteers by long term care ombudsman programs: The effectiveness of recruitment, supervision and retention. Washington, DC: The National Association of State Units on Aging, The National Center for State Long Term Care Ombudsman Resources.

This study of volunteers used in long term care ombudsman programs in 46 states, outlines the extent of volunteer use, factors influencing staffing decisions, the success of substate programs, how states manage and support the use of volunteers, and how substate programs manage volunteers. The findings indicate which programs are not successful and that assistance in recruitment is the most important program need.

73.   U.S. Senate Special Committee on Aging, American Association of
        Retired Persons, Federal Council on the Aging, & U.S. Administration
        on Aging. (1991). Aging America: Trends and projections. Washing-
        ton, DC: U.S. Department of Health and Human Services.

        This publication is the latest edition that provides national data on the
        status of older Americans and the aging of that population. Based on
        secondary data, the subject of volunteering is included as a social
        characteristic in chapter 6. Results from the May 1989 Current
        Population Survey are utilized in order to show the characteristics of
        volunteer workers, as well as the type of volunteer work performed, by
        age group.

74.   Vaillancourt, Francois, & Payett, Micheline. (1986, Oct-Dec). The
        supply of volunteer work: The case of Canada. Journal of Voluntary
        Action Research, 15(4), 45-56.

        This article is included because it gives a national picture of volunteer-
        ing in Canada. Data by age are given, showing participation by age
        and gender, as well as, the likelihood of doing volunteer work, by age
        and gender. This first national view of volunteer behavior in Canada
        indicates results similar to those observed in other North Atlantic
        societies.

75.   Ventura-Merkel, Catherine, & Worthy, Edmund H. (1982). Voluntary
        action and older Americans: A synthesis of significant data. Washing-
        ton, DC: National Council on the Aging.

        Using the written materials from five national studies, this report
        synthesizes the results of these surveys and was produced to highlight
        some of the significant findings. The following subjects are covered:
        participation rates by demographic variables, non-participants as part
        of the potential volunteer force, types of volunteer activity and future
        research issues and needs.

76.   Ventura-Merkel, Catherine, & Worthy, Edmund, Jr. (1982). Volun-
        tary action and older Americans: Findings of seven national surveys.
        Washington, DC: National Council on the Aging.

77.   Walsh, Elaine. (1986). Volunteerism among the elderly: A secondary
        analysis of a national survey. (Doctoral dissertation, Fordham
        University, 1986). Dissertation Abstracts International, 48, 483A.

Based on secondary analysis of the 1981 national random cross sectional survey by NCOA and conducted by Louis Harris with an N of 1,837, this work showed that less than 9 percent of the variance in volunteer status could be explained by the demographic and background variables used in the study. It is suggested that health and income are predictors of both volunteer activity and life satisfaction, but that volunteerism is not a predictor of life satisfaction among the elderly.

78.   Worthy, Edmund H. Jr., & Ventura-Merkel, Catherine. (1982). Older volunteers: A fact sheet (SUDOCS No. HE23.3002:01 1\3) Washington, DC: National Council on the Aging.

This publication is a summary of the 1974 and 1981 NCOA/Louis Harris national surveys giving the data that pertains to volunteer behaviors. The focus of the many tables is to show the changes that have occurred over the seven years between the surveys with emphasis on number and proportion of volunteers, demographic characteristics of the volunteer force, and reasons for volunteering.

Chapter 3
Empirical Studies

Social and Psychological Characteristics of Older Volunteers

79.   Aalami-Rad Mahvash. (1986). Self-actualization levels among retired senior citizens who do or do not engage in volunteer services. Dissertation Abstracts International, 47, 1701B.

Utilizing a static-group comparison, this study investigated differences in self-actualization levels among 97 elderly retirees who were grouped according to number of hours of involvement per week in social services. Data analysis revealed no significant differences among the groups, nor between those who were involved in both social services and leisure activities and those not involved in such activities.

80.   Benson, Peter, Dohority, John, Garmon, Lynn, Hansen, Elizabeth, Hochschweder, Martha, Lebaod, Carol, Rohr, Roberta, & Sullivan, Jane. (1980). Intrapersonal correlates of non-spontaneous helping behavior. Journal of Social Psychology, 110, 87-95.

This is a general article which examines the correlates of nonspontaneous helping behavior. Although the subjects used were students, it is of interest that the best predictors were social responsibility norms, intrinsic religion, and locus of control.

81.   Bull, C. Neil. (1983, November). The relationship between voluntary
        association participation, volunteering and mood. Paper presented at
        the 36th annual meeting of the Gerontological Society of America, San
        Francisco, CA.

        This paper looks at the relationship between the time spent in voluntary
        association participation and life satisfaction as measured by the
        multiple affect adjective checklist (MAACL) using a national sample of
        1543 adults in the USA (273 aged 65+) collected by the Gallup
        Organization in 1982. Controlling for health, income, and gender,
        volunteer participation does not significantly add to satisfaction.

82.   Elderly residents in Ontario: Their participation as volunteers and their
        interest in volunteerism. (1985). Ontario: Minister for Senior Citizens
        Affairs Seniors Secretariat.

        This short paper is the result of a survey of a random sample of 846
        elderly in Ontario looking at actual and potential participation rates.
        Correlates of participation such as ethnic background, income, gender
        education, as well as reasons and type of volunteer work preferred, are
        given

83.   Fischer, Karla, Rapkin, Bruce D., & Rappaport, Julian. (1991).
        Gender and work history in the placement and perceptions of elder
        community volunteers. Psychology of Women Quarterly, 15(2), 261-
        279.

        A sample of 169 RSVP members, with a mean age of 73.3 years, was
        utilized in this study examining the patterns of job perceptions of
        female versus male volunteers in two types of volunteer positions:
        those involving and not involving leadership roles.   Significant
        interaction effects were found with regard to the independent variables
        "gender" and "leadership."

84.   Fischer, Lucy Rose, Mueller, Daniel P., Cooper, Phillip W., & Chase,
        Richard A. (1989). Older Minnesotans: What do they need? How do
        they contribute? St. Paul, MN: Amherst H. Wilder Foundation.

        Based on approximately 1,500 interviews with elderly Minnesotans (age
        60 and older) this statewide survey represents the first study in nearly
        20 years of Minnesota's senior citizens.   Topics covered include:
        demographic characteristics, income and poverty, living arrangements,
        housing and transportation needs, health and functional ability, social
        ties, and voluntary activities. Seventy million hours per year is the

current estimated amount of time devoted by Minnesota's elderly to voluntary services.

85.   Goodman, Catherine Chase. (1984). Natural helping among older adults. The Gerontologist, 24, 138-143.

Age-segregated housing developments were used to study the patterns of natural helping among a sample of 67 respondents who were mainly white women in their mid-70's. A topology of three neighborhood exchange types is formed from the data: high helpers, who exhibit a quasi-professional style of helping but without reciprocation, mutual helpers, who show a style of both give and take, and isolates, whose social ties and help supports are outside of the neighborhood.

86.   Hamilton, Frederick & Schneiders. (1988). Attitudes of Americans over 45 years of age on volunteerism. Washington, DC: American Association of Retired Persons.

Included in this publication are the partial results of a telephone survey of 2,001 Americans over 45--only those questions dealing with volunteerism are included--and a comparison of trends in volunteerism from a 1981 AARP survey.

87.   Hunter, K. I., & Linn, Margaret W. (1980-81). Psychosocial differences between elderly volunteers and non-volunteers. International Journal of Aging and Human Development, 12, 205-213.

In this frequently cited article, the authors present the findings of a study which compared forty-nine non-volunteers over age sixty-five, and fifty-three volunteers, within the same age category, who currently provided services to the Veterans Administration Hospital in Miami, Florida. Demographic and health-related data were collected and seven dimensions of psychosocial adjustment were measured. Findings indicate that the volunteers had a significantly higher degree of life satisfaction, a stronger will to live, and fewer symptoms of depression, anxiety and somatization, than non-volunteers. The authors advise caution, however, in generalizing the results.

88.   Kelly, Lynn S. (1989). Life satisfaction and happiness in older volunteers in the North Carolina Agricultural Extension Service. (Doctoral dissertation, North Carolina State University, 1989). Dissertation Abstracts International, 50, 1179A.

A comparison of 182 older volunteers (50 years and older) with 71 younger volunteers showed differences in demographic, socioeconomic and participation characteristics between these two groups. Levels of life satisfaction, happiness, and value orientation were also found to be different as were rates of participation, with age influencing satisfaction with volunteering.

89.   King, Anthony E. O., & Gillespie, David F. (1985, Fall). Administrative lessons from volunteer profiles. The Journal of Volunteer Administration, 4(1), 28-37.

A descriptive study based on 1,346 respondents who were either current or former volunteers in the American Red Cross (ARC) is reviewed. Although all ages were covered--ranging from 16 to 97 years with a mean of 45 years--this article is useful as a general article which looks at the demographics of volunteers, how they learned of volunteer opportunities, the degree of enjoyment in their work and the skills acquired during their volunteer experience.

90.   Kozak, D., & Degar, J. (1982). Elderly volunteers in the service of the elderly [Special issue]. The Gerontologist, 22, 208-209. Abstract of paper presented at the 35th annual meeting of The Gerontological Society of America.

The purpose of this qualitative study was to compare and determine the characteristics of elderly volunteers who volunteer to serve an older population with those serving a younger or heterogeneous population. The findings indicate that it is the job responsibilities that determine which population is served rather than a preference to work with a specific population.

91.   Lee, Alec J., & Catherine Burden. (1990-91, Winter). Understanding the needs of the senior volunteer. The Journal of Volunteer Administration, 9(2), 13-17.

Through a telephone survey of 258 Greater Victoria (British Colombia) residents, the characteristics of seniors who volunteer and their reasons for doing so are explored. Data are given on the kinds of volunteer work performed, reasons for becoming involved in volunteering, as well as, reasons for not volunteering.

92.   Lucas, Linda L. (1990). A comparison of older adult volunteers and non-volunteers: An empirical test of Human Capital Theory. Unpublished master's thesis, Colorado State University, Fort Collins, CO.

This study which compares twenty-seven volunteers with twenty-six non-volunteers found no significant differences between these groups either on formal characteristics or on any of the several human capital variables. Also, the study describes those aspects of volunteer work that provide the greatest satisfaction for the older volunteers, using a volunteer satisfaction index.

93.   Mellinger, Jeanne, & Holt, Robert. (1982). Characteristics of elderly participants in three types of leisure groups. Psychological Reports, 50, 447-458.

145 participants in three types of programs were interviewed: 30 as volunteers in RSVP, 45 as part of recreation programs, and 70 at nutrition sites. Volunteers were found to be highly active and service-oriented but with fewer social contacts and placing less value on social services. Recreation participants were less active and nutrition participants least active.

94.   Morris, Robert, & Mass, Scott. (Eds.). (1988). Retirement reconsidered: Economic and social roles for older people. New York: Springer.

The greater part of this book focuses on the economic roles of older people and the types and frequency of employment. However, there are references to volunteering showing (in Chapter 9) that those who continued to work, when compared with retirees, performed about the same amount of volunteer work. In addition, Chapter 16 looks at the concept of service credits and how and where they have been used.

95.   Ozawa, Martha N., & Morrow-Howell, Nancy L. (1986, October). Elderly volunteers and the time they contribute: An empirical study [Special issue]. The Gerontologist, 26, 117A-118A. Abstract of paper presented at the 39th annual meeting of The Gerontological Society of America.

Human capital theory is used in this study to predict the characteristics of senior volunteers who spend more time providing services than do others. The data shows that those elderly with good physical functioning, psychological adjustment and social resources were more likely to be volunteers. Perceived health of participants was the best predictor of time spent volunteering.

96.   Ozawa, Martha N. (1986, January). Case management services by the volunteer elderly: The Final Report. St. Louis, MO: Washington

University, The George Warren Brown School of Social Work. (NTIS No. SHR 0113878 XAB. 8704)

In this final report, a program in St. Louis is evaluated to see if the program mobilized and trained elderly volunteers to become "case managers" serving other elderly persons. The study found that those volunteers who ranked highly on four human capital variables were, as predicted, better managers. However, because of inadequate professional support, volunteers became overwhelmed by difficult cases and turnover was high.

97.   Ozawa, Martha N., & Morrow-Howell, Nancy. (1988). Services provided by elderly volunteers: An empirical study. Journal of Gerontological Social Work, 13(1-2), 65-80.

In trying to predict whether an elderly volunteer is a provider of instrumental services, this study of 63 volunteers finds that when looking at the level of physical and mental strengths of elderly volunteers, their perceived health is a significant predictor, as is level of education and number of elderly persons served. On the whole, elderly volunteers prefer socialization and reassurance over instrumental services.

98.   Perry, William H. (1982). A study of older volunteers in Leon County, Florida. (Doctoral dissertation, Florida State University, 1982). Dissertation Abstracts International, 43, 549A.

A comparison of volunteers (N=75) with non-volunteers (N=56) shows that in this study, volunteers had more income, were younger, were more educated and more likely to be white and married. The volunteers also had higher levels of self-esteem and peer relations. Both volunteers and non-volunteers stated that they would prefer to work and serve members of their own peer group.

99.   Roberts, B. L., Chatterjee, B. F., Diangi, P., & Tinsley, R. J. (1986, October). Characteristics of elderly volunteering for research [Special issue]. The Gerontologist, 26, 69A. Abstract of paper presented at the 39th annual meeting of The Gerontological Society of America.

One of the few studies that have looked at the characteristics of persons who are elderly and volunteer as subjects for research is outlined in this paper. The study finds that older subject volunteers are younger, more physically and mentally healthy, functionally intact and involved in social activities than their non-volunteer counterparts.

100.   Stone, J., & Velmans, E. (1980). Retirees as volunteers: An evalua-
        tion of their attitudes and outlook. Volunteer Administration, 13(4), 4-
        8.

Motivations

101.   Brady, E. Michael, & Fowler, Mary Lee. (1988).   Participation
        motives & learning outcome among older learners.   Educational
        Gerontology, 14, 45-56.

        The Elderhostel program is examined in this article using 560 older
        students to evaluate self-reported learning outcomes and to determine
        the reason for participation. These elderly students showed growth in
        humanities/critical thinking, as well as human relations/personal
        development. The best predictor of learning was the setting of goals.

102.   Cohen-Mansfield, Jiska. (1989). Employment and volunteering roles
        for the elderly: Characteristics, attributions, and strategies. Journal of
        Leisure Research, 21(2), 214-227.

        Workers and volunteers in a sample of 81 males and 88 females in
        northern Israel, were compared with non-workers and non-volunteers
        looking at the reasons given for either activity or inactivity. Also
        examined, were strategies used to find work or a volunteer job by this
        group of elderly. In addition, the interchangeability of these two roles
        is discussed.

103.   Dorfman, Lorraine T., & Moffett, Mildred M. (1987).   Retirement
        satisfaction in married and widowed rural women. The Gerontologist,
        27, 215-221.

        Included in this study, which examined the correlates of retirement
        satisfaction in married and widowed rural women, are the variables of
        voluntary organizational participation and the performance of volunteer
        work. A positive increase in both voluntary organizational participation
        and volunteer work were related to two measures of satisfaction: the
        Retirement Descriptive Index and the Life Satisfaction Index-Z.

104.   Gillespie, David F., & King, Anthony E. O. (1985, December).
        Demographic understanding of volunteerism. Journal of Sociology and
        Social Welfare, 12, 798-816.

        In this article concerning 1,346 American Red Cross volunteers, the
        variable "age" is used to look at differences on nine major reasons
        given for volunteering. Compared with the younger volunteers, the
        older volunteers indicated in much larger numbers (differences of up
        to 22%) that they volunteered "to help others."

105.   Ilsley, Paul J. (1990). Enhancing the volunteer experience: New
        insights on strengthening volunteer participation, learning, and
        commitment. San Francisco: Jossey Bass.

        This general work looks at the understanding of volunteering from the
        perspective of the volunteer, the factors that shape the quality of the
        volunteer experience, and the use of volunteers' insights in order to
        strengthen volunteer programs. Included are the use of volunteers in
        long-term care settings.

106.   Kay, Bonnie. (1984). Barefoot doctors in rural Georgia: The effect of
        peer selection on the performance of trained volunteers. Social Science
        and Medicine, 19, 873-878.

        While not confined to older volunteers, this useful article outlines a
        study showing that volunteer emergency medical coordinators in 36
        rural Georgia communities, who were selected by their peers, were
        used as first responders at a significantly higher rate. The notion that
        a selection process, managed and controlled by a local organization
        which screens and eliminates candidates, makes a strong positive
        impact on volunteer performance.

107.   Kelly, Joan. (1981, Summer). Seniors talk about why they volunteer.
        Generations, 5(4), 18-19.

        The three major ACTION programs (Foster Grandparent, Senior
        Companion and RSVP) are examined in this article through the eyes of
        approximately 1,000 older volunteers. Anecdotal evidence is given
        which demonstrates 1) the many reasons why these volunteers continue
        in their roles and 2) the positive feedback they receive.

108.   Lee, Alec J., & Burden, Catherine. See entry number 91.

109.   Lee, Alec J., & Burden, Catherine. (1991, Summer). Volunteering
        activities of seniors. The Journal of Volunteer Administration, 9(4),
        29-35.

        This follow-up study to the original (Lee and Burden, 1990-91 see
        entry number 91) continues the original investigation of the nature and
        extent of volunteer participation among Greater Victoria's senior
        citizens. This work provides greater detail concerning: 1) the nature
        of volunteer work performed, 2) motivation for volunteering, 3)

reasons to (or not to) volunteer, and 4) effective/ineffective recruit-ment strategies.

110.   Luciani, Johnelle. (1992). Motivational determinants of volunteer behavior: A logistic regression analysis using between-group and within-group triangulation techniques. Unpublished doctoral disserta-tion, Philadelphia: University of Pennsylvania.

In an attempt to investigate the initial motives of the elderly to volunteer in human service settings, samples of 244 elderly volunteers and 188 nonvolunteers, from five eastern states, were compared through the use of both qualitative and quantitative techniques in a post facto design. Similarities/differences between the two groups with regard to demographic characteristics, psychosocial traits, and motives to volunteer were explored using three major theories of adaptation to aging: disengagement, activity, and continuity, with some support emerging for the latter two. Significant differences between the two groups were found with regard to the following variables: marital status, education, income, employment status, in addition to reciprocity and employment-related motives.

111.   Midlarsky, Elizabeth, & Kahana, Eva. (in press). For the sake of others: Altruism and helping by the elderly. Newbury Park, CA: Sage.

After two theoretical chapters, one dealing with altruism and the second, the major conceptual models used in gerontology, this book examines the nature, antecedents and ramifications of helping by older adults. Evidence is summarized which indicates that helping is a valued activity and one that is frequently engaged in by the older population.

112.   Miller, P. R. (1982). Are older volunteers different? Paper presented at the 35th annual meeting of the Gerontological Society of America, Boston. The Gerontologist, 22(5), 208.

With the use of data from 200 volunteers in agencies in the Baltimore-DC area, this study investigates motivation, satisfaction, training, and staff/management/volunteer acceptance. The results show that there are different reasons why older people volunteer and that their expectations differ from those previously reported. Volunteers are selective of both task and agency and desire increased responsibilities, more involvement with staff, and greater participation in decision making.

113.   Moore, Larry (Ed.). (1985). <u>Motivating volunteers: How the rewards of unpaid work can meet people's needs</u>. Vancouver, BC: Vancouver Volunteer Centre.

Scattered throughout this book of papers are several references to some of the motivations for volunteering among the older population. This is a good general reference book as an introduction to the subject of the motivations of volunteers.

114.   Morrow-Howell, Nancy, & Mui, Ada. (1989). Elderly volunteers: Reasons for initiating and terminating service. <u>Journal of Gerontological Social Work</u>, <u>13</u>(3,4), 21-34.

Using a sample of 83 older volunteers trained to perform two major functions--instrumental support and referral--it was found that for females, the reasons for volunteering were both altruistic and social, while for males they were altruistic only. In the sample, the major reason for quitting was the volunteer's inability to help as much as they thought they would.

115.   Perkinson, Margaret A. (1990). Conceptual and methodological issues in socialization research: Studying socialization to volunteer roles in a multipurpose senior center. <u>Dissertation Abstracts International</u>, <u>51</u>, 607A.

Data collected on socialization of older adults to volunteer roles in a midwest multipurpose senior center are used to look at guidelines for deriving standards or criteria by which to direct an individual's socialization to given norms. Social norms are distinguished from statistical norms, and other methodological issues are outlined.

116.   Rehm, Priscilla. (1981). Volunteers: Another endangered species? <u>Graduate Woman</u>, <u>75</u>(3), 21-24.

In this general article about the role of women as volunteers, the author looks at the history of volunteerism, the five major reasons why women volunteer, and the growing role of the retiree in helping others.

117.   Roadburg, Alan. (1981). Perceptions of work and leisure among the elderly. <u>The Gerontologist</u>, <u>21</u>(2), 142-145.

In this article, interviews with 245 elderly respondents were used in an examination of their perceptions of work and leisure. Among those activities mentioned as work, volunteering was placed in that category by 13 percent of the women but none of the men. Among those activities mentioned as leisure, 3 percent of the women viewed volunteering as such, while less than one percent of the men perceived volunteering to be a leisure activity.

118.   Robins, Arthur J., Kabrick, Rodman P., & Frautschi, Nanette M. (1981). Use of critical incidents for planning, implementing and evaluating a training program for foster grandparents. Educational Gerontology, 7, 111-122.

The training of sixteen Foster Grandparents is the subject of this article where the training needs were assisted by task performance analysis procedures including the critical incident technique. The training focused on the role of the volunteer in helping develop socially acceptable behavior in their charges. An evaluation showed that volunteers highly rated by supervisors improved with training. Others did not.

119.   Stevens, Ellen S. (1988). Goodness-of-fit in senior volunteerism: Correlates of role satisfaction and retention. (Doctoral dissertation, Columbia University, 1988). Dissertation Abstracts International, 49, 2812A.

To study the differential rates of retention of older volunteers, 151 current and former senior volunteers were studied. The role of the quality of recognition, interaction with others, and continuity of respect were found to be associated with higher levels of satisfaction and retention.

120.   Stevens, Ellen S. (1989-90, Winter). Utilizing a "rich" resource: Older volunteers. The Journal of Volunteer Administration, 8(2), 35-38.

This brief article presents findings from a study of 151 older volunteers on senior volunteer retention and satisfaction, noting that "feeling useful" appeared to be the predominant motivation for volunteering, whereas "not feeling useful" was the most frequently cited reason for ceasing to volunteer. Practical applications, directed toward volunteer administrators, are also offered and include sections on recruitment practices, placement practices, and supervision.

121.   Vineyard, Sue. (1984, Spring). Recruiting and retaining volunteers: No gimmicks, no gags! The Journal of Volunteer Administration, 2(3), 23-28.

Barriers

122.   Allen, Kenn K. (1981, Summer).   The challenges facing senior
        volunteering. Generations, 5(4), 8-9, 56.

        In this article, the author speculates about whether there will be enough
        older volunteers to meet a growing demand.   Evidence presented
        suggests that older volunteers may be opting out of the direct service
        role because they cannot afford it.

123.   Cnaan, Ram A., & Cwikel, Julie G. (1991).   Elderly volunteers:
        Assessing their potential as an untapped resource.   Manuscript
        submitted for publication.

        Many policy analysts and researchers consider the elderly to be an
        untapped source for volunteer recruitment and this paper identifies the
        origins of this societal expectation and its actualization. Presented, in
        addition, are analyses of factors contributing to and deterring the actual
        deployment of large numbers of elderly as volunteers.

124.   Helfand, Lynn, McKay, Hunter, & Meiners, Mark R. (1990, Septem-
        ber). The Robert Wood Johnson Foundation Service Credit Banking
        Projects: A survey of program development experience.   Paper
        presented at the 1990 annual meeting of the American Public Health
        Association, New York, New York.

        In 1987 The Robert Wood Johnson Foundation provided three year
        grants to six sites to implement a program using service credit banking
        which allows elderly volunteers to help other elders stay in their homes
        and at the same time, provide for their own future needs. This paper
        examines the experiences of each site after three years and includes
        discussion of the obstacles met and how they were overcome.

125.   Offut, D., & Kim, P. (1980, October). Life perception and problems
        of senior volunteers [Special issue]. The Gerontologist, 20, 173.
        Abstract of paper presented at the 33rd annual meeting of The
        Gerontological Society of America.

        Using 125 RSVP members, this study looks at life satisfaction, amount
        of volunteer hours, distance from volunteer station, as well as volunteer
        experience and problems. The authors recommend that to improve
        retention the following actions be taken: improve transportation,
        minimize bureaucratic sanctioning behavior and provide regular
        preventative health care for the volunteers.

126.   Pasquel, Zulma Marie Keynton. (1986). <u>Recruitment and retention of
        older volunteers</u>. Unpublished master's thesis, Virginia Polytechnic
        Institute and State University, Blacksburg.

        Based on a total of 171 elderly respondents from three different
        samples, this study looks at the factors that relate to the recruitment and
        retention of volunteers. The data shows that personal contact, present
        participation, family or friend benefiting from organization, and senior
        newsletter were the best recruitment strategies, while utilization of
        expertise, flexible schedules, placement in a position of expertise, the
        acquisition of new skills, and training were most important for
        retention.

127.   Perry, William. (1983). The willingness of persons 60 or over to
        volunteer: Implications for the social services. <u>Journal of Geronto-
        logical Social Work</u>, <u>5</u>(4), 107-118.

        Older persons have historically been under-utilized as volunteers and
        this study found that among 56 non-volunteers, 59 percent expressed
        a willingness to volunteer. However, the main reason given for not
        doing so was that no one had asked them. Illness and poor health, lack
        of transportation and being too busy were also given as important
        reasons for not volunteering.

128.   Rydberg, Wayne D., & Peterson, Linda J. (Eds.). (1980). <u>A look at
        the eighties: Crucial environmental factors affecting volunteerism</u>.
        Appleton, WI: Aid Association for Lutherans.

        This very informative publication is based on the research papers of
        four respected experts in the field of volunteerism whose task was to
        look at environmental factors that will affect the future of volunteerism.
        Although not focusing solely on older volunteers, this publication
        reports that the subjects of inflation, energy use, lifestyles, technology,
        corporate involvement and litigation are very important for the field of
        volunteerism.

Impact of Volunteering on Older People and Volunteers

129.   Ager, Charlene L. (1986, Winter). Therapeutic aspects of volunteer
        and advocacy activities. Physical and Occupational Therapy in
        Geriatrics, 5(2), 3-11.

        Explored in this review paper are three avenues of volunteering by the
        elderly: self-help groups, community service, and advocacy. The
        therapeutic value of being a volunteer is outlined and special attention
        is given to the role of the occupational therapist in facilitating such
        activities.

130.   Barber, Putman. (1981, Summer). Volunteering: Community can't
        survive by cash alone. Generations, 5(4), 10-11.

        The author of this brief essay discusses both the benefits of volunteer-
        ing, and more importantly, the great amount of informal, spontaneous
        volunteering that may not be included in sociological/statistical analyses
        but which, nonetheless, greatly improves the quality of life for
        countless Americans. A brief review of ACTION programs is
        provided as well.

131.   Borman, Leonard, & Lieberman, Morton. (1981). Impact of self-help
        groups on widows' mental health. National Reporter, 4(7), July, 2-5.

132.   Butler, Robert N., & Gleason, Herbert P. (Eds.). (1985). Productive
        Aging: Enhancing vitality in later life. New York: Springer.

        In chapters 5 and 6 of this edited volume, there is a discussion of the
        role that volunteerism plays in the decisions to work past retirement.
        Being a volunteer is seen as a viable alternative to work and an activity
        that can give psychological meaning to life.

133.   Chambré, Susan Maizel. (1984). Is volunteering a substitute for role
        loss in old age? An empirical test of activity theory. The Gerontolo-
        gist, 24, 292-298.

        A test of the view that volunteering can provide a means of acquiring
        substitutes for the loss of certain roles--work or family--is examined in
        this article. The findings suggest that role loss does not significantly
        influence volunteering. Rather, the variables of socioeconomic status
        and gender have a greater impact.

134.   The children's museum. (1981, July-Aug). Aging, 319-320, 42.

This one page review discusses the outcomes of senior volunteer involvement in a children's museum. Outlined are the types of activities that the older volunteers participate in and the benefits for both generations.

135.   Criss, William Robert. (1987). The effects of volunteer activity on psychosocial adjustment among the elderly. Unpublished master's thesis, University of Central Florida, Orlando.

Using 27 older volunteers and 37 persons without volunteer experience as controls, pre and post tests after two months of volunteer activity, this study looked at the effect of volunteering on psychosocial adjustment. Analysis of covariance with repeated measures showed no significant improvement in subjective well being between the two groups using measures of self-esteem, life satisfaction, sense of control, optimism, anxiety, and depression. The major factor responsible for the lack of treatment effect was traced to initial high adjustment scores prior to volunteer participation.

136.   Fengler, Alfred. (1984, June). Life satisfaction of subpopulations of elderly: The comparative effects of volunteerism, employment, and meal site participation. Research on Aging, 6(2), 189-212.

A study of 1400, systematically selected elders in a needs assessment survey encompassing a four county area of New England, is used to examine the relationship between elders, who are volunteers, employed, or participating in meal site programs, and life satisfaction. The findings show that those with the greatest number of resource deficits benefitted most from participation. However, those disadvantaged elders who participated as a volunteer in the RSVP program showed the most consistent, positive relationship with life satisfaction.

137.   Fogelman, Charles F. (1981, Summer). Being a volunteer: Some effects on older persons. Generations, 5(4), 24-25; 49.

This article begins by utilizing a quasi-experimental design in a comparative examination of current, versus aspiring, volunteers. Using the OARS Methodology, this study indicates that the volunteers benefit socially, emotionally, and physically, but not necessarily economically. Also of interest, are the respondents' responses to predictions of 1) their expectations of the volunteer experience and 2)their perceptions of recipients' needs.

138.   Getze, Linda H. (1981, Aug-Sept). Are you helping others? <u>Modern Maturity</u>, <u>24</u>(4), 49-51.

       The ways in which millions of retirees are finding satisfaction in volunteer work are outlined in this article, with examples of the types of volunteer jobs available included. A short list of contact agencies for prospective volunteers is presented at the conclusion of the essay.

139.   Harel, Zev, & Lindenberg, Ruth Ellen. (1981). Community service opportunities and older Americans. <u>Journal of Sociology and Social Welfare</u>, <u>8</u>(1), 111-121.

       The authors of this article offer a review and discussion of the benefits of contributory roles for older Americans and outline various contributory opportunities available to this segment of the population, such as: community service employment programs, sponsored volunteer programs, and associations of the elderly.

140.   Janeway, Elizabeth. (1990, June-July). Everyday heroes. <u>Modern Maturity</u>, <u>33</u>(3), p.40-45, 95.

       This general article uses case histories of older volunteers in several national programs to illustrate why volunteers appear to get more out of life. These examples demonstrate 1) how volunteers learn new skills and increase their health and 2) the variety of opportunities available.

141.   Kornblum, Seymour F. (1981). Impact of a volunteer service role upon aged people. (Doctoral dissertation, Bryn Mawr College, Graduate School of Social Work and Social Research, 1981). <u>Dissertation Abstracts International</u>, <u>43</u>, 267A.

       Data from 198 older people who responded to a search for RSVP participants and who were divided into three groups: those who volunteered, those who did not volunteer, and those who dropped out of the volunteer role within six months, is the subject of this study. Participation as a volunteer had no clear and measurable impact on health, morale, social participation or self perception. Differences that did appear were attributed to self-selection.

142.   Lackner, Robin, & Koeck, Cynthia. (1980, December). <u>The elderly as Resource: An examination of volunteerism among the elderly in Minnesota</u>. St. Paul: Minnesota State Planning Agency, Human Resources Planning.

This technical report describes the various activities in which elderly volunteers engage with emphasis on: 1) the types of groups involved in volunteerism, and 2) the effect of volunteering on the older volunteer, agencies, clients, and the government. The major issues surrounding volunteerism and the impact of the changing populations on volunteer behavior are discussed.

143.   Lindeman, Bard. (1988). Three cheers for older heroes. <u>50 Plus</u>, <u>28</u>(3), 4-5.

This short editorial essay outlines cases in which volunteering has greatly impacted an particular elderly individuals' lives.

144.   McDonald, Anne Elizabeth (1988). The effects of work/non-work orientations on morale among retired workers in Bridgeport, Connecticut. (Doctoral dissertation, Pennsylvania State University, 1987). <u>Dissertation Abstracts International</u>, <u>49</u>, 919A.

With the use of a sample of 220 retired adults--participants in Senior Centers and RSVP programs compared with non-participants--this work looks at Continuity Theory to test the relationship between continuity and morale. Support was not given to such a relationship with the major impact on morale being gender, income and health.

145.   McLaughlin, Frank. (1983). See entry number 70.

146.   Maillet, Michael Paul. (1987). <u>A comparative analysis of retired senior volunteers on life satisfaction and volunteer satisfaction in a border city</u>. Unpublished master's thesis, University of Texas at Arlington.

The attitudes of Mexican-American (N=64) and Anglo (N=62) elderly RSVP volunteers are compared in this study, with the focus on the relationship between volunteering and life satisfaction. The data shows that participation was not positively related to life satisfaction for either group. However, for Mexican-American volunteers, the need to be needed was the most important indicator of volunteering.

147.   Mellor, Joanna M., Rzetelny, Harriet, & Hudis, Iris E. (1981). Self-help groups for caregivers of the aged. In <u>The Natural Supports Program, Strengthening informal supports for the aging: Theory, practice and policy implications</u> (pp. 52-59). New York: Community Service Society.

Self-help groups are the subject of this chapter in a monograph on strengthening informal supports for the aging. After a review of the self-help group approach, case histories are used to illustrate the continuum of self-help groups and the role of leaders and facilitators. Some of these self-help groups are composed of the elderly helping the elderly.

148.   Midlarsky, Elizabeth. (1988, December). Helping and volunteering by the elderly: The role of perceived opportunity. Washington, DC: AARP Andrus Foundation.

A Solomon Four-Group design was used on 120 elderly respondents to measure the outcome of providing information in both verbal and written formats, on prosocial volunteer opportunities in the community. The experimental data indicates the intervention significantly affected perceptions of opportunities to be of service, and actual helping behavior, and that respondents preferred receiving information both face-to-face and in brochures.

149.   Milligan, Sharon, Maryland, Patricia, Ziegler, Henry, & Ward, Anna. (1987). Natural helpers as street health workers among the black urban elderly. The Gerontologist, 27, 712-715.

The results of a 5 year experience in which volunteers, mostly elderly, in a black urban community provided geriatric health outreach are outlined in this article. This outreach program enhanced the service organizations and showed that volunteers can be recruited and trained to assist families in the monitoring of the well-being of frail elderly.

150.   Newman, Sally, Vasudev, Jyotsna, & Onawola, Roland. (1985, December). Older volunteers' perceptions of impacts of volunteering on their psychological well-being [Special issue: Aging and mental health]. Journal of Applied Gerontology, 4(2), 123-127.

151.   Rouse, John T. (1982). Life satisfaction of the elderly as volunteer social support providers. Dissertation Abstracts International, 43, 1305B.

This study found no significant difference in life satisfaction between 65 volunteers, actively involved in either the Foster Grandparent Program or the Senior Companionship Program, and 48 non-volunteers who were on the waiting lists of both programs. Findings did reveal, however, significant correlations between health, age, and number of hours per week volunteered and life satisfaction. These three variables were likewise found to be the best predictors of life satisfaction. In addition, clinical interviews were utilized among selected high and low scorers on the Life Satisfaction Index Z with the purpose of improving the quality of measurement of this variable.

152.   Smith, Christen G. (1985). Relationships between selected meanings of leisure, volunteering, and work of senior center program participants. (Doctoral dissertation, Texas Woman's University, 1985). Dissertation Abstracts International, 46, 1736A. (University Microfilms No. 85-16737)

The meanings of leisure, volunteering, and work as seen by 26 volunteers and 22 non-volunteers drawn from a sample of senior centers, is the subject of this work. Using the semantic differential section of the "Study of Leisure," form 0769, the author found significant differences between the groups, with volunteers showing a positive relationship with respect to the connotative meaning of the concepts.

153.   SRA Technologies, Inc. (1985). Senior companion program impact evaluation: Final Report (Contract No. 83-043-1007). Washington, DC: Action.

This evaluation of the Senior Companion Program is based on data collected over the five year period 1979 to 1984 using in-person interviews. The report looks at the impact of becoming a volunteer, remaining in the program, and the impact upon clients. In addition, a set of recommendations is provided.

154.   Stevens, Ellen S. (1991). Toward satisfaction and retention of senior volunteers. Journal of Gerontological Social Work, 16(3-4), 33-41.

In the Fall of 1985 and again in the Spring of 1987, 151 senior volunteers completed questionnaires focusing on volunteer satisfaction as well as personal and role characteristics. The study found that 75% were continuing to serve and that those likely to be more satisfied were those who a) had a history of volunteering, b) perceived congruence between volunteer role expectations and actual job experiences, c) had contact with others and d) perceived recognition and appreciation.

155.   Vachon, M. L. S., Lyall, W. A. L., Rogers, J., Freedman-Letofsky, K., & Freeman, S. J. J. (1980, November). A controlled study of self-help intervention for widows. American Journal of Psychiatry, 137, 1380-1384.

A two year study of 162 widows in Toronto paired 68 with a widow contact who had participated in a training seminar which examined problems of bereavement, support counseling, and the spectrum of community resources. The findings, when compared with the control group of 94 widows, shows that the differences at the follow-up times of 1, 6, 12 and 24 months indicate that those receiving counseling followed the same general course of adaptations, but at an accelerated rate.

Chapter 4
Settings

Educational Institutions

156. Aday, Ronald H., Rice, Cyndee, & Evans, Emile. (1991). Intergenerational Partners Project: A model linking elementary students with senior center volunteers. The Gerontologist, 31, 263-266.

A nine month intergenerational program is described which was established to bring about more intimate involvement between a group of 4th graders and senior volunteers. The format used is presented, and ongoing activities as well as program benefits are described.

157. Angelis, Jane. (1990, Jan-Feb). Bringing old and young together. Vocational Education Journal, 65(1), 19-21.

Outlined in this brief article are the necessary steps for establishing intergenerational programs in the classroom setting. Addressed specifically are: 1) needs assessment, 2) job description, 3) recruitment, 4) screening, 5) orientation and training, 6) recognition, and 7) evaluation.

158. Baggett, Sharon. (1981). Attitudinal consequences of older adult volunteers in the public school setting. Educational Gerontology, 7, 21-31.

Forty-five children in kindergarten through grade three were paired with elderly volunteers-recruited from senior centers and nutrition projects-to form an experimental group. Using the Children's Attitude Toward the Elderly (CATE) test and a matched control group, pre and post scores showed no significant attitude changes in the treatment group in which each child spent 2 hours per week with the elderly person.

159.   Banerjee, Neela. (1988). Older and wiser: An intergenerational drop-out prevention effort. New York: Interface.

This report outlines the history and obvious success of an intergenerational program in the city of New York which uses older volunteers to reduce the dropout rate in high schools. A successful and expanding program is profiled and recommendations for replication offered.

160.   Barrett, Dennis, Myers, Renee, Kramer, Cynthia, Newman, Sally, & Mullins, June. (1985). Intergenerational volunteer program in special education: A manual for implementation. Pittsburgh, PA: Pittsburgh University, Allegheny Intermediate Unit. (ERIC Document Reproduction Service No. ED 271 926)

Designed primarily as an aide to assist special education administrators and teachers in the development of an intergenerational school volunteer program, this manual provides the following: 1) background information on the existing program--located in Allegheny County (Pennsylvania), 2) a listing of specific benefits derived from the program, 3) identified concerns of both teachers and volunteers, as well as answers to such concerns, 4) extensive program implementation quidelines, and 5) a resource list and bibliography.

161.   Boone, J. (1980). Volunteering: A two way street in East St. Louis. American Education, 16, Jan-Feb, 19-27.

162.   Broadbent, JoAnne D. (1986). A study of children's ability to identify the elderly and desire to be with the elderly as a result of interaction with senior volunteers in the preschool classroom. Dissertation Abstracts International, 46, 3241A.

With a pre and post-test, seventy children between the ages of three and four years who were enrolled in child care centers were used as an experimental group and compared with a control group of sixty children. The treatment was to use female RSVP participants to assist in classrooms from one to sixteen weeks. No differences were found in the children's ability to identify the elderly or desire to interact with the elderly.

163.   Campanale, Eugene A. (1984, Summer).   Students and adults caring for each other. College Student Journal, 18(2), 140-142.

The author of this short article suggests that colleges and universities provide living accommodations on or near campuses to house retired professionals, faculty, or business people who in turn would volunteer their services to the educational institutions. Such intergenerational contact is seen as having benefits for both the students and retirees.

164.   Carney, John M., Dobson, Judith E., & Dobson, Russell L. (1987, March). Using senior citizen volunteers in the schools. Journal of Humanistic Education and Development, 25(3), 136-143.

165.   The children's museum. (1981, July-Aug). Aging, 319-320, 42.

This one page review discusses the outcomes of senior volunteer involvement in a children's museum. Outlined are the types of activities that the older volunteers participate in and the benefits for both generations.

166.   Clarke, Raymond E. (1984). The development of a model program for the recruitment, training, and utilization of elderly school volunteers. Dissertation Abstracts International, 46, 58A.

From the data collected using both a survey instrument (in twenty-four school districts) and nine on-site interviews, information was provided to complete a model program intended to be utilized for the recruit-ment, training, and use of older volunteers in schools. The model is outlined in a clear and detailed handbook but not tested.

167.   Colledge, Nancy J., & Wurster, Stanley R. (1985, December). Intergenerational tutoring and student achievement. Reading Teacher, 39(3), 343-346.

This is a short article which looks at the Volunteer Partners Program--a program that solicits, trains, places and then evaluates retired people as volunteers in public schools. A pre-post test, with a control group, examined the outcome of the use of tutors for grades 2-12, finding significant gains in reading but non-significant gains in math and grammar.

168.   Courson, Frances H., & Heward, William L. (1989, May). Using
         senior citizen volunteers in the special education classroom. Academic
         Therapy, 24, 525-532.

         The many advantages of utilizing senior volunteers in the special
         education classroom setting are described in this article which includes
         brief sections on 1) recruitment, 2) using volunteers effectively, 3)
         retention of volunteers, 4) planning assignments, and 5) ensuring
         volunteer satisfaction.

169.   Dear, Annette E., Thurlow, Martha L., & Ysseldyke, James E. (1987,
         September). Adults in the classroom: Effects on special education
         instruction. University of Minnesota, Monograph No. 8. Instructional
         Alternatives Project. Washington, DC: Office of Special Education and
         Rehabilitative Services. (ERIC Document Reproduction Service No.
         ED 293 270)

         The impact on the instructional process of having paraprofessionals and
         adult volunteers--especially parents and senior citizens--in special
         educational classrooms is reviewed using the current literature. The
         review suggests a need to continue the use of this valuable resource.
         However, roles must be specified, volunteers told of their responsibili-
         ties, and teachers trained in terms of how to best use both parents and
         volunteers.

170.   De Phillis, Susan. (1982, July). Recruit "Grandpeople" as volunteer
         tutors, and students will reap the rewards. The American School Board
         Journal, 169(7), 28-30.

         The author outlines how an elementary school in Riverside, California,
         when faced with budget cuts, turned to senior citizens as volunteers.
         A detailed history of the project is given, as well as a very useful set
         of hints on how to start a similar project.

171.   Dickerson, Ben E., Myers, Dennis, & Seelbach, Wayne. (1984).
         Educational brokerage: A mechanism for establishing elders as
         educators. Educational Gerontology, 10, 349-356.

         The under-utilization of elders as resources in universities, colleges and
         the community is the subject of this work. The reasons for this lack of
         use are reviewed and an educational brokerage system--a case study--is
         outlined with a focus on retired faculty.

172.   Dickson, Gloria Ann. (1990). <u>Senior citizens as instructional mentors to enhance the secondary school curriculum</u> (Doctoral dissertation, Texas A&M University, 1990). Dissertation Abstracts International, <u>51</u>, 1492A.

The use of older volunteers in secondary schools is the subject of this study. A 76.2% response rate from 319 Texas secondary school principles provides data which show that three-fourths of the schools had volunteer programs, with less than half using older volunteers. Most programs were small and less than one-third used volunteers in teaching roles. However, principles strongly supported the idea of using older volunteers as instructional mentors.

173.   Freedman, Marc. (1988). <u>Partners in growth: Elder mentors and at-risk youth</u>. Philadelphia, PA: Public/Private Ventures. (ERIC Document Reproduction Service No. ED 303 561)

Using a qualitative methodology, this study looked at five ongoing intergenerational programs to develop an understanding about how relationships form, who benefits from such relationships--the youth and/or the elderly--does bonding take place, and do these programs stimulate such relationships? Site visits, conferences, and interviews with practitioners and academics were all used to produce the report.

174.   Gundling, Robert. (1986). <u>Bridging the gap between generations: An intergenerational program between a public school, senior center and two private nursing facilities</u>. Fort Lauderdale, FA: Nova University. (ERIC Document Reproduction Service No. ED 281 670).

The predominantly favorable results of a practicum which involved senior volunteers with the students, teachers and parents in a Pottstown, Pennsylvania public school are reported in this article, which includes examples of classroom materials used in the program.

175.   Helping kids: The ripple effect. <u>(1987). Aging</u>, <u>355</u>, 28.

This short review of an RSVP program in Monroe, Michigan describes how a small program has grown to a staff of 30 tutors who work with 90 children in 5 schools.

176.   Hettling, Lillian B. (1983, March-April). <u>Chronicles: An intergenerational experience, aged volunteers in 8th grade</u>. Aging, <u>337</u>, 26.

Reviewed in this short article is a program in Yorktown Heights, New York called "Chronicles" in which older volunteers are used to bring social studies courses to life.

177.   Jellison, Holly. (1980). Higher education and the older volunteer: A place for everyone. Washington, DC: American Association of Community and Junior Colleges.

This seventy-three page monograph on models of older adult volunteer programs consists of thirteen articles written either by or with information provided by program staff and volunteers. Included are two appendices, one containing brief descriptions of four other volunteer programs, and the other, locations and telephone numbers of various senior citizen college programs.

178.   Kramer, Cynthia, & Newman, Sally. (1985). Senior citizen school volunteer program: A manual for program implementation. Albany, NY: Center for the Study of Aging.

This manual is based on the intergenerational model developed by Generations Together and tested in over 75 schools. After reviewing the background of the program, specific attention is placed on implementation, maintenance, and evaluation. Excellent, detailed instructions on recruitment, training workshops, handouts, and evaluation tools are provided as well.

179.   Lowenthal, Barbara, & Egan, Rosemary (1991). Senior citizen volunteers in a university day-care center. Educational Gerontology, 17, 363-378.

A pilot study was conducted to involve senior citizen volunteers with preschool children in a university day-care setting with the dual objective of enhancing the children's reading readiness and fostering relationships between seniors and young children. Pre and post questionnaire results indicate some positive results occurring in the experimental group.

180.   McClusky, Howard Y., & Brahce, Carl. (1982). Comparative support roles for older volunteers and non-volunteers in school learning activities. The Gerontologist, 27(5), 195. Abstract of paper presented at the 35th annual meeting of the Gerontological Society of America, Boston.

Adult volunteers, ages 60 and over were compared with volunteers in non-school projects, as well as with non-volunteers. The study showed that there were differences between these three groups and many comparisons are given. For example, being with friends was important for both volunteer groups but not for the non-volunteers. School volunteers were least interested in knowing about public assistance.

181.   Marks, Ronald E. (1981).   Children's perceptions of the elderly: A quasi-experimental study of attitudes and attitude change. (Doctoral dissertation, University of Pittsburgh, 1980).   Dissertation Abstracts International, 41, 5245A.

182.   National School Volunteer Program. (1986).   Guidelines for involving older school volunteers.   Alexandria, VA: Author.

This publication offers a good, well thought out set of guidelines which cover the topics of needs assessment, recruiting, placement, orientation, training, and support of older volunteers used in multiple roles in schools. Special problems associated with the program, used in seven cities, are outlined. Illustrations of some of the announcements and forms used are provided as well.

183.   Newman, Sally, Vasudev, Jyotsna, & Baum, Martha. (1983, August). The Experience of senior citizen volunteers in intergenerational programs in schools and the relationship to life satisfaction: Final report.   Pittsburgh: University of Pittsburgh, Center for Social and Urban Research.

This study describes the experience of older volunteers in intergenerational programs in schools. Examined is the relationship between their experience and their life satisfaction. Data collected from 350 volunteers at three sites showed no significant difference on a life satisfaction scale between new and experienced volunteers, possibly due to self selection. However, qualitative data strongly support that: school volunteering contributes to other aspects of satisfaction such as improved feelings about oneself and positive feelings and gratification associated with participation in the programs.

184.   O'Connor, Darlene M. (1987).   Elders and Higher Education: Instrumental or expressive goals? Educational Gerontology, 13, 511-519.

Although volunteering is not the focus of this article, it is included to illustrate studies that have looked at the learning goals of older adult students. This study shows that elders were more likely to consider learning "for its own sake" (expressive goals) rather than instrumental outcomes as the most important reason for their participation.

185.   Positive research on use of older people in preschool programs. (1983-84, Dec-Jan). Aging, 342, 42-43.

A study of intergenerational research carried out by the Ethel Percy Andrus Gerontological Center is outlined in this short article, with a focus on the use of older volunteers in preschool programs. The study found that the presence of older people benefitted preschool programs by increasing the number of adults in the classroom, improving the quality of education, saving money, and enhancing preschool programs in the community.

186.   Powers, Sally, & Snyder, Joan. (1982, October). Project LOVE (Let Older Volunteers Educate) [Special issue]. The Gerontologist, 22, 208. Abstract of paper presented at the 35th annual meeting of the Gerontological Society of America.

This project looks at the effects of older volunteers working in an elementary school on the childrens' attitudes toward old people. Pre- and post-tests comparing the control with the experimental group shows that the childrens' attitudes were positively affected on: the 24-item attitude scale, their dexriptions of older people, and their responses to the question, "Do you want to get old?"

187.   Pratt, Fran. (1984, Aug-Sept). Teaching today's kids--tomorrow's elders. Aging, 346, 19-26.

This general review article focuses on several intergenerational programs which utilize older volunteers in school throughout the United States. The author examines the effect of these volunteers on school curricula and

188.   Pritchard, David, & Tomb, Karyl. (1981). Emerging new service roles for older adults on college and university campuses. Educational Gerontology, 7, 167-175.

Utilizing basic data gathered from a survey of 65 higher education institutions out of a population of 200, in which a 33% response rate was obtained, this article explores and describes the extent to which programs have been initiated to involve older adults in meaningful volunteer tasks. The study indicates that there are major barriers to the implementation of such programs; however, 21 cases were identified in the United States.

189.   Ross, Lorraine N., & Lidoff, Lorraine. (1984). <u>Senior volunteer literacy tutors</u>. Washington, DC: National Council on the Aging.

This handbook focuses on a model in which older volunteers are used to help non-English speaking community residents with conversational English. A step-by-step process is outlined dealing with the assembly of resources, implementation procedures, training, funding, resource materials (used or available) and sample forms.

190.   Schreter, Carol. (1991, February). Older volunteers. <u>The American School Board Journal</u>, <u>178</u>(2), 35-36.

This brief article discusses the ways in which older volunteers in intergenerational programs do more than just build bridges between the old and young. The author demonstrates that the use of older volunteers can build political support for the schools as well. Outlined are instructions for setting up programs and the national organizations that can be of assistance.

191.   Senior tutors help the public schools. (1984, June-July). <u>Aging</u>, <u>345</u>, 30-31.

This brief article reviews a program in Tacoma, Washington called RAISE (Retirees Active in Student Education) outlining the types of activities introduced into the schools.

192.   <u>Senior volunteer literacy tutors</u>. (1984). Washington, DC: National Council on the Aging.

193.   Springer, I. (1989). Helping 'em get it right: Reward for older classroom volunteers is watching their pupils succeed. <u>AARP Bulletin</u>, <u>30</u>(11), 16.

194.   Strickland, Charlene. (1990, December). Intergenerational reading: Encouraging the grandlap. <u>Wilson Library Bulletin</u>, <u>65</u>(4), 46-48, 164-165.

A review of several library programs that have successfully used the older volunteer to assist with intergenerational reading programs is at the heart of this short article. The major subjects covered are: finding and using volunteers, illustrations of "kits" available, and descriptions of several programs.

195.   Tierce, Jerry Wood, & Seelbach, Wayne C. (1987, Jan-Feb). Elders as school volunteers: An untapped resource. Educational Gerontology, 13, 33-41.

This paper reviews the role and scope of school volunteerism and suggests ways to integrate RSVP participants into school volunteer programs, especially the National School Volunteer Program (NSVP). A useful overview is made of the role responsibilities in school programs with emphasis upon the RSVP director, volunteer coordinator, school principal, teacher, and volunteer.

196.   Walls, Nancy. (1987). Three generations of love. Aging, 355, 2-5.

Bringing together the Foster Grandparent Program with the Teenage Parent Alternative School Program (TPASP) in a suburb of Detroit, is the focus of this article which discusses student eligibility and the ways in which the older volunteers work in the child-care center of the program.

197.   Weinschenk, Doris. (1986). I and R service from volunteer senior citizens. Library Journal, 111(17), 50.

The use of older volunteers in a library setting in Nassau County, New York is reviewed in this short article. The volunteers were used in the I and R capacity. The volunteers completed 15 months of training in the use of the library and its computer. To assist in this program's replication, a video, volunteers handbook and training manual are available.

198.   Yarmon, Morten. (1981). Never too old to teach. 50 Plus, 21(11), 58.

This short essay focuses on the elderly who continue to participate in the educational system, either as paid workers or volunteers. Reviews of 1) the levels of the educational system served, and 2) the types of volunteer organizations that help provide teaching opportunities, are provided.

Health Care Institutions

199.   Biegel, David E., & Napersteck, Arthur J. (Eds.). (1982). See entry
        number 5.

200.   Blumenfield, Susan, & Rocklin, Carol. (1980). Senior counselor-
        assistants for a geriatric program in a community hospital. Social
        Work in Health Care, 6, 89-100.

        In a 300 bed acute care geriatric hospital, a program using 9 senior
        volunteers is outlined showing the rationale for the program and the
        recruitment issues that had to be overcome prior to the selection
        process. The training of the volunteers is discussed as is the manner
        in which they were integrated into the hospital system. Evaluation of
        the program showed that for younger patients and those with the
        greatest length of stay, the volunteers were more helpful.

201.   Board of Social Ministry & World Relief. (n.d.). Ministry: Guidelines
        for nursing home volunteers. (Available from [Project Compassion,
        Inc., 3455 Woodward Ave., Detroit, MI 48201-2799]).

        A short monograph explaining the need for visiting those in nursing
        homes begins this guide which then sets out guidelines for volunteers
        covering such practical matters as length of stay, talking versus
        listening, gift giving, doing errands, and providing, when necessary,
        devotional activities.

202.   Brickner, Philip W., Harnett, Ellen R., Hillman, Deborah Jay, &
        Schrarer, Linda K. (1985). Project HELP (Homebound Elderly Linked
        with Peers): Final report to the Robert Wood Johnson Foundation.
        New York: PRIDE Institute, Department of Community Medicine, St.
        Vincent's Hospital and Medical Center.

        This report covers the evaluation of a demonstration project funded by
        the Robert Wood Johnson Foundation from 1983 to 1985. The purpose
        of the project was to provide older volunteers as caregivers for the
        homebound elderly. The report covers major facets of the program:
        recruitment, matching of volunteers with clients, supervision, costs,
        volunteer recognition, and program outcomes. A cost analysis showed
        that per visit costs were low, but substantial efforts were required to
        identify and recruit volunteers.

203.   Brummel, Steven W. (1984, Winter).   Senior Companions: An
        unrecognized resource for long term care.   Pride Institute Journal of
        Long Term Home Health Care, 3(1), 3-12.

204.   Campbell, Ruth, & Chenoweth, Barbara. (1981).   Health education as
        a basis for social support.   The Gerontologist, 21, 619-627.

        The "Peer Support System" is a program operating out of an outpatient
        geriatric clinic in which 48 peer counselors were recruited and trained
        to conduct monthly health education workshops.   The project served
        2,500 people over a two year period in the health clinic, at a low
        income nutrition site, in a rural community, and in a nursing home.
        Very positive evaluations were found in these diverse settings.

205.   Crose, Royda, Duffy, Michael, Warren, Judith, & Franklin, Betty.
        (1987, June).   Project OASIS: Volunteer mental health paraprofes-
        sionals serving nursing home residents.   The Gerontologist, 27, 359-
        362.

        To meet the emotional needs of the elderly in nursing homes, the
        demonstration program outlined in this article used older adult
        volunteers and trained them to be mental health paraprofessionals.
        With the use of case studies, details are given on the recruitment,
        training, and supervision of these volunteers.

206.   Franklin, Betty, & Smith, Bert Kruger. (1986).   OASIS for the old.
        Austin, TX: The University of Texas, Hogg Foundation for Mental
        Health.

        An evaluation of the Older Adults Sharing Important Skills (OASIS)
        project is the purpose of this short monograph.   The primary goal of
        the project was to provide paraprofessional mental health services to
        nursing home residents.   An historical review of the program is
        followed by an evaluation of the outcomes of the project on the nursing
        home clients and the older volunteers.

207.   Granger, Vincent, & Sherwood, Clarence. (1983).   Discharged
        rehabilitation patients: Impact of follow-up surveillance by a friendly
        visitor.   Archives of Physical Medicine and Rehabilitation, 64, 346-
        353.

        A well planned study looking at the impact of using a friendly visitor
        to check on patients after discharge from a hospital is the subject of this
        article.   An examination of three groups: those who received friendly

visitors and biannual nursing visits, biannual nursing visits only, and a control group, revealed no meaningful pattern of differences between groups on any of the outcome measures.

208.   Halpert, Burton P. (1988). Volunteer information provider program: A strategy to reach and help rural family caregivers. The Gerontologist, 28(2), 256-259.

The Volunteer Information Provider Program, a successful train-the-trainer program that uses volunteers to help caregivers in providing home health care to the rural elderly, is reviewed in this article. Reasons for the program's success, why and how volunteers were used, and how the program tapped into previously existing networks, are reviewed.

209.   Halpert, Burton P., & Sharp, Tessa S. (1989). A model to nationally replicate a locally successful rural family caregiver program: The Volunteer Information Provider Program. The Gerontologist, 29, 561-563.

The Volunteer Information Provider Program (VIPP)--a rural family caregiver program first tested in Missouri and now used nation-wide--is outlined in this article showing the strategy used, as well as the key elements to the success of the program. A total of 657 professionals and volunteers were utilized to aid 7,213 rural family caregivers. This successful program shows that a local project can be transplanted over state lines.

210.   Hayes, Christopher. (1983, Jan-Feb). Using older adults as peer counselors. Aging, 335-336, 32-34.

Project PACE (Psychological Alternative Counseling for Elders), a Santa Anna, California program, which has recruited 28 older volunteers to help with peer counseling, is reviewed in this article. The operation of this program, its outcomes, and successes are described in detail.

211.   Heller, Barbara R., Walsh, Fredrick J., & Wilson, Kathleen M. (1981). Seniors helping seniors: Training older adults as new personnel resources in home health care. Journal of Gerontological Nursing, 7, 552-555.

A total of 250 older adults were enrolled in a program (Seniors Helping Seniors) to train home health care workers to act as community resources for the elderly. This article outlines the content of the five events taught and evaluates retention and action six months after completion of training.

212.   Holmes, Elizabeth A., & Everline, Diane. (1984). The use of volunteers in social group work as remotivation leaders. The Journal of Long-Term Care Administration, 12(4), 9-12.

The remotivation program, in existence for more than ten years at the National Lutheran Home, is described in this article. Mainly older volunteers are trained in five all-day seminars in remotivation techniques and after leading twelve sessions, are certified. Special groups for males and those who suffer from cognitive dysfunction are described, as well as evaluative procedures which are used every six months. It was found that staff support is essential to the success of the program.

213.   The Hospital Research and Educational Trust. (1981). Innovative utilization of older persons in volunteer service programs: Six hospitals report on model projects. Chicago: Author.

This volume is a good introduction to the use of volunteers in hospital settings. Emphasis is placed upon: developing volunteer programs, profiling of volunteers, assessing program outcomes, and benefits for the volunteer, community, and hospital. Discussions of program development problems, as well as the extension of programs to other settings, are presented. Six case histories are covered in detail.

214.   Kay, Bonnie. (1984). See entry 106. Social Science and Medicine, 19, 873-878.

215.   Kirkpatrick, Royce V., & Patchner, Michael A. (1987, Summer). The utilization of peer counselors for the provision of mental health services to the aged. Clinical Gerontologist, 6(4), 3-14.

This is a short but useful article focusing on how an agency can prepare for the use of peer volunteer counselors to assist the elderly. The subjects covered are recruitment, training and retention. There is, in addition, a review of the types of services that can be provided to the elderly.

216.   May, David, McKeganey, Neil, & Flood, Mary. (1986, September). Extra hands or extra problems? Volunteers for the domiciled, elderly mentally infirm. Nursing Times, 82(36), 35-36, 38.

The collapse of a program which utilized volunteers as visitors for home-bound dementia patients is used to illustrate the difficulty of using volunteers with these types of patients. Several problems arose: a lack of volunteers, patients not remembering the volunteer from visit to visit and thus not allowing them in the house, and resistance from the family caregiver who viewed the visits as a criticism of their role.

217.   Milligan, Sharon, Maryland, Patricia, Ziegler, Henry, & Ward, Anna. (1987). Natural helpers as street health workers among the black urban elderly. The Gerontologist, 27, 712-715.

The results of a 5 year experience in which volunteers-mostly elderly-in a black urban community provided geriatric health outreach, are outlined in this article. This outreach program enhanced the service organizations and showed that volunteers can be recruited and trained to assist families in the monitoring of the well-being of frail elderly.

218.   Milwaukee's Volunteer Guardian Program. (1984). Aging, 347, 25-27.

This short article reviews the Volunteer Guardian Program, through which older volunteers are used to assist approximately 2,500 persons--without family--who reside in nursing homes and county institutions. Useful information is given on recruitment, training, and the evaluation of this successful and needed program.

219.   Nagel, Joseph, Cimbolic, Peter, & Newlin, Margie. (1988, January). Efficacy of elderly and adolescent volunteer counselors in a nursing home setting. Journal of Counseling Psychology, 35(1), 81-86.

This study looks at the effects of a volunteer training program on the depression levels of nursing home residents. Two groups, each consisting of 20 volunteer counselors (10 elderly and 10 adolescent) were trained separately. The experimental group was trained in empathetic listening, while the control group was given information about the aging process. The results indicate that residents who received a volunteer counselor improved the level of depression, regardless of the type of training received by the volunteers, nor was age of the volunteer important.

220. Netting, F. Ellen, & Kennedy, Ludell N. (1985). Project RENEW: Development of a volunteer respite care program. The Gerontologist, 25, 573-576.

The development and implementation of an in-home respite program using trained volunteers to provide at-home companionship and supervision for the frail elderly is reviewed. The data support the problem that even though there were requests for help, out of forty-eight requests, twenty potential recipients refused the service. The reasons for such rejections are outlined and some good suggestions made to overcome this and other problems.

221. Netting, F. Ellen. (1990, Summer). Volunteerism and community building in continuing care retirement communities. The Journal of Volunteer Administration, 8(4), 25-34.

Examined in this article are the volunteer roles and relationships that formed in four retirement communities in Arizona. Interviews with volunteer coordinators and 25 volunteers allowed for four major types of volunteers to be identified. A number of programmatic and research questions are also raised.

222. Nursing home residents join RSVP. (1981, Jan-Feb). Aging, 315-316, 35-37.

This article shows how 300 residents of a Maryland nursing home joined the Retired Senior Volunteer Program (RSVP). The many varied volunteer roles--both within and outside the nursing home--are described.

223. Omoto, Allen M., & Snyder, Mark. (1990, March). Basic research in action: Volunteerism and society's response to AIDS. Personality and Social Psychology Bulletin, 16(1), 152-165.

The importance of the use of volunteers to assist AIDS patients is reviewed in this excellent article. The antecedents of the decision to volunteer, the experiences of the volunteers and the recipients, as well as the consequences for these volunteers is outlined.

224. Payne, Barbara P., & Bickley, Marea Jo. (1980). Volunteering and mental health. In E. R. Crawford & L. H. Keating (Eds.). Exploring mental health parameters (Vol 3). Atlanta, GA: Atlanta Regional Commission.

Focusing on the relationship between volunteering and mental health, both with respect to the volunteer and the recipient, this chapter includes sections on: who volunteers and why, a definition and discussion of mental health, a preventative/interventive mental health model of volunteering, the volunteer experience (positive and negative effects on mental health), and the implications of the model.

225. Ross, Lorraine N. (Ed.). (1984). <u>Compendium of health promotion-related initiatives for older adults</u>. Washington, DC: National Council on the Aging.

Under the four topical areas of injury control, nutrition, physical fitness and appropriate drug use, this compendium of health-promotion related initiatives is used to show the range of interests and capacities among national voluntary organizations who have the elderly as their major clientele.

226. RSVP brings volunteering to nursing homes. (1982, Jan-Feb). <u>Aging</u>, <u>323-324</u>, 32-33.

This article reviews the benefits acquired through the use of fifty older volunteers who are residents of two nursing homes in the Gainesville, Florida area. Through the help of RSVP, these volunteers serve as welcoming committees to new residents, do friendly visiting, deliver mail and assist in craft projects. The article notes that the use of volunteers appears to tap into the cooperative spirit and help maintain local involvement.

227. Sander, Pamela. (1989). <u>Activity and volunteer service policies and procedures</u>. Houston, TX: M & H.

This is a manual to be used by activity coordinators to aid in setting up volunteer programs in nursing homes. The manual is divided into three major sections: required procedures (in terms of job description and documentation), activity and volunteer information (regarding activity planning and volunteer services), and delivery of social services via referral.

228. Shannon, Barbara, Smickes-White, Helen, Davis, Barbara, & Lewis, Christine. (1983). A peer educator approach to nutrition for the elderly. <u>The Gerontologist</u>, <u>23</u>, 123-126.

A nutrition education program using 22 older volunteers who completed 95 training sessions with 933 participants is described. The participants reported that the sessions were well organized and interesting and provided useful information.

229.   Snyder, Mark, & Omoto, Allen M. (In Press). Who helps and why? Volunteerism and society's response to AIDS. In S. Spacapan & S. Oskamp (Eds.), Helping and being helped in the real world: The Claremont Symposium on Applied Social Psychology. Newbury Park, CA: Sage

Expanding on their previous work, (see entry number 223) the authors again look at the process model they use in their attempt to understand volunteering with AIDS patients. The three major components of the model deal with the antecedents of volunteering, the experiences of the volunteers, and the consequences of volunteering--with an emphasis on changes in attitudes, knowledge and behavior.

230.   Warner, J. A. (1981). Nursing home residents become school volunteers. Nursing Homes, 30(4), 20-23.

231.   Ziegler, Suzzane, & Kind, Johanna. (1982). Evaluating the observable effects of Foster Grandparents on hospitalized children. Public Health Reports, 97, 550-557.

The use of Foster Grandparents as parent-surrogates in an acute care setting in Toronto is evaluated in this study. The 67 children in the study were divided into three groups: Foster Grandparent (N=26), undervisited control (N-21), and parent-visited (N=20). Observation on five behavioral variables found no significant differences between either of the three groups.

232.   Zischka, Pauline C., & Jones, Irene. (1984). Volunteer community representatives as ombudsmen for the elderly in long-term care facilities. The Gerontologist, 24, 9-12.

A program for the training of volunteer ombudsmen to act as advocates on behalf of residents of long-term care facilities is outlined. Discussions of both the content of the training program, as well as the recruitment of volunteers are presented following a description of the programs beginnings. Illustrations of ombudsmen interventions are provided, with special emphasis on problems of recruitment and retention.

Religious Institutions

233.   Bock, Kathy (Ed.). (1990). Volunteers - The hands, head, and heart
       of a Shepherd's Center. Kansas City, MO: Shepherd's Centers of
       America.

       Intended for directors or organizers of Shepherd's Centers, this
       publication addresses many practical aspects covering recruitment,
       training, supervision, coordination, recognition, and burnout.

234.   Johnson, Kenneth G., & Schiaffino, Virginia. (1990). A follow-up
       study in 1990 of projects in The Robert Wood Johnson Foundation's
       Interfaith Volunteer Caregivers Program (1984-1987). (Available from
       [National Federation of Interfaith Volunteer Caregivers, Inc., 105
       Mary's Avenue, P.O. Box 1939, Kingston, NY 12401]).

       This is a short report that outlines the major statistics of the follow-up
       to the 25 projects funded to recruit and train volunteers from faith
       congregations in order to help serve disabled persons. Over 50 percent
       of these volunteers were over the age of 60, while 92 percent of those
       served by the program were also 60 years of age or older. Outlined
       are: the places where the referrals for the program originated, the
       types of services offered, and the important factors conducive to
       producing a successful caregiver program.

235.   Marshall, Maxine. (1981). How we became a more caring congrega-
       tion. Nashville, TN: Discipleship Resources.

       In this monograph book about how to involve a congregation in church
       activities is a good chapter (chapter iv) about involving the elderly in
       volunteering and how to match talent with opportunity, as well as, on
       the job support.

236.   Marshall, Maxine. (1980). Volunteers: Hope for the future. Nash-
       ville, TN: Discipleship Resources.

       This short guide is to be used by churches to recruit, train and keep
       volunteers. Outlined are the major reasons for volunteering, means of
       developing volunteers, and creating and maintaining a support system.

237.   Maves, Paul B. (1981). Older volunteers in church and community:
       A manual for ministry. Valley Forge, PA: Judson.

Written and produced by older adults, this manual focuses primarily upon the ministry of older potential volunteers. It is divided into two sections: perspectives on the ministry of older volunteers and managing volunteer ministries with older people. However, several chapters contain useful information regarding elderly volunteerism in general.

238.   Schreck, Harley Carl. (1985). Helping the needy elderly in urban America: An analysis of volunteerism in strengthening neighborhood support systems for homebound elderly persons in Seattle, Washington. (Doctoral dissertation, University of Washington, 1984). Dissertation Abstracts International, 45, 3395A.

The use of a volunteer church-based network to provide at-risk elderly in Seattle, Washington with a variety of in-home services is studied. Nearly half of the volunteers were themselves elderly and the data indicate that the program built neighborhood support systems to help the "truly needy" who were seen by the volunteers as fellow community members.

239.   Takamura, Jeanette C. (1991, Fall-Winter). Dana is joy: A volunteer caregivers' program in the Buddhist tradition. Generations, 15(4), 79.

This article is a short review of a project in Honolulu that addresses the needs of the frail and homebound elderly through assistance by volunteers--many of whom are elderly themselves. The project is undertaken in a non-sectarian setting but based on the Buddist religion and the concept of "dana" or selfless giving.

240.   Thomopoulos, Elaine, Roos, Christine, & Ellor, James W. (Eds.). (1985). Organizing a volunteer program serving the elderly. (Available from [C.A.N., 4840 W. Byron St., Chicago, IL, 60641]).

This manual is an edited collection of chapters to be used by clergy and lay leaders as an aid in setting up programs to service the elderly--especially in large urban areas. Step by step instructions are given, based upon experiences in Chicago, with a focus on: needs assessment, recruiting, training, publicity, fundraising, evaluation, and where to look for technical assistance.

241.   Van Wert, Johanna. (1989). Interfaith volunteer caregivers: A special report. Princeton, NJ: Robert Wood Johnson Foundation.

This special report is a review of the 25 Interfaith Volunteer Caregivers Projects funded by the Robert Wood Johnson Foundation during the period 1983 to 1986. The use of interfaith coalitions allowed for the recruitment of volunteers--11,000 from 900 congregations who provided assistance to some 26,000 frail elderly. All age groups were used as volunteers.

242.   Wilson, Marlene. (1983).   How to mobilize church volunteers. Minneapolis: Augsburg.

Although the elderly are not the central focus of this work, it is important because it gives a step-by-step process regarding the involvement of church volunteers, many of whom will be elderly. The book covers the topics of: why to become involved, how to assess present conditional practices, what actions can be taken, how to overcome obstacles, and how to deal with outreach.

243.   Wuthnow, Robert, Hodgkinson, Virginia A., & Associates. (1990). Faith and Philanthropy in America: Exploring the role of religion in America's voluntary sector. San Francisco: Jossey-Bass.

Although this excellent collection of articles has as its focus, the relationship between religion and giving--mainly financial--there are several chapters that include the time spent volunteering. Attention is drawn to Chapter 7 which looks at Jewish giving patterns and presents data showing little relationship between giving and volunteering. The concluding chapter examines the future of giving and volunteering.

Chapter 5
National Programs

Roles for Retired Professionals

244.   Brody, Robert. (1985). Giving time, sharing knowledge. 50 Plus, 25(6), 68-69.

The author of this short essay discusses a program, funded by Dow Chemical and called SERV (Service Effort for Retiree Volunteers), in which the company's retirees are farmed out and matched to provide volunteer help in multiple settings.

245.   Chetkow-Yanoov, Benyamin. (1986). Leadership among the aged: A study of engagement among third-age professionals in Israel. Ageing and Society, 6, 55-74.

This study, which focuses upon the characteristics of elderly professionals who both remained active during their third-age and functional as leaders, presents some interesting findings and recommendations relevant to volunteerism. The author suggests that as sixty-eight percent of the identified leaders engaged in volunteerism in addition to salaried work, governmental bodies, as well as voluntary service organizations, would be wise to utilize potential pools of elderly volunteer leaders.

246.   Friedman, Judith A. (1989). Retired professional social workers as
        volunteers: An exploratory study. (Doctoral dissertation, Barry
        University, School of Social Work, 1988). Dissertation Abstracts
        International, 49, 3157A.

        A sample of 357 retired professional social workers was surveyed in
        order to compare and contrast the characteristics of those who do
        volunteer with those who do not. Support for continuity theory showed
        that the volunteer group had a higher rate of prior volunteering, was
        healthier, female, and reported greater life satisfaction and altruism.

247.   Frykman, Elma. (1981, Summer). A senior volunteer project in the
        corporate sector. Generations, 5(4), 41.

        This short review of the success of a corporate volunteer program--the
        Honeywell Retirees Volunteer Project (HRVP)--highlights the impor-
        tance of these types of programs, not only for the retiree, but for the
        community at large.

248.   Hougland, James G., Jr., Turner, Howard B., & Hendricks, Jon.
        (1988, July-Dec). Rewards and impacts of participation in a gerontolo-
        gy extension program. Journal of Voluntary Action Research, 17(3-4),
        19-35.

        Retired professionals (N=39) were made available as volunteers to
        public service agencies and were followed during the stages of their
        participation. Through training by the Gerontology Extension Project
        (CED) in Kentucky, 147 presentations were made by these volunteers
        to 59 different agencies. The data indicates that the participants
        responded positively, but not dramatically to this type of social
        participation.

249.   Jecklin, Mary Jean, & Fetter, Elizabeth A. (1985). Needs of older
        employees and retirees: Task force results of the Corporate Volunteer-
        ism Council of Minneapolis and St. Paul, Minnesota. St. Paul, MN:
        Honeywell, Inc. (ERIC Document Reproduction Service No. ED 265
        285)

        This publication presents the results of a two-part study sponsored and
        conducted by the Corporate Volunteerism Council (CVC) of Minneapo-
        lis and St. Paul, with the objective of identifying and addressing the
        needs of its retirees and older employees. Twenty-five CVC members
        responded to a survey, identifying "emotional needs" as the greatest
        unmet need of the elderly. In addition, 10 male and 10 female retirees

participated in moderated focus group discussions designed to address the emotional and socialization needs of the elderly--with an emphasis on volunteering as a strategy to meet those needs.

250.   Kirby, Judy. (1984). Work after work. London: Quiller.

This book is a review of the history of the REACH (Retired Executives Action Clearing House) as well as a more general look at volunteerism in Great Britain. The major topics covered are: placement of volunteers in work situations or as volunteers, the major charity organizations in Britain, examples of community and international placement, and three excellent indexes of voluntary organizations in that country.

251.   Nellis, Elwyn A. (1989). A SCORE that counts: The story of the Service Corps of Retired Executives. Rockville, MD: Reproductions, Inc.

The first twenty-five years of the SCORE Program is reviewed, looking at its early history, the middle years, its present form, and goals. Also reviewed are some of the major crises the organization has had to overcome.

252.   Nusberg, Charlotte. (1984). Volunteer opportunities for senior scientists and engineers (SSE): In the Washington, DC metropolitan area. Washington, DC: American Association of Retired Persons.

253.   Soll, Harriet P. (1982, May-June). SCORE: Volunteerism at its best. Aging, 327-328, 24-26.

This article reviews a very successful program--SCORE (Service Corps of Retired Executives). With a membership of nearly 8,500, retired executives--in a person-to-person advisory relationship--provide talent to assist male businesses. Good examples of the outcomes of this program are provided.

254.   Vinokur-Kaplan, Diane, & Bergman, Simon. (1986, Summer). Retired Israeli social workers: Work, volunteer activities, and satisfaction among retired professionals. Journal of Gerontological Social Work, 9(4), 73-86.

In a sample of retired professional social workers, this study found a gradual withdrawal from paid work and an increase in volunteering.

Satisfaction with retirement was related to health, income and work status.

Foster Grandparent Program

255.   Anisfeld, E., & Mayer, M. (1985, October). Postpartum support by
        Foster Grandparents of mothers at risk of child maltreatment [Special
        issue]. The Gerontologist, 25, 240. Abstract of paper presented at the
        38th annual meeting of The Gerontological Society of America.

        The use of Foster Grandparents to assist young postpartum mothers
        considered at risk is outlined in this paper. Using a quasiexperimental
        design and based on data from 14 dyads, the findings indicate that
        relationships between the Foster Grandparents and postpartum mothers
        can be sustained. However, there is, as yet, inconclusive evidence
        about the impact of this program on the mother-child relationship.

256.   Ashby, Vicki R. (1981). Foster Grandparents teach Indian lore and
        language. Children Today, 10(3), 16-17.

        A Foster Grandparent Program, utilized in an effort to keep Native
        American traditions alive at two tribal centers in the state of Washing-
        ton, is described in this article.

257.   Foster Grandparent transforms aged mental patient. (1980, Nov-Dec).
        Aging, 313-314, 40-41.

        This short article outlines the history of how an older mental patient
        was able to become a Foster Grandparent to two mentally retarded
        children. The benefits to both generations are presented as well.

258.   Grandparents go to jail. (1984, June-July). Modern Maturity, 27(3),
        p. 104.

        This brief article describes how the Foster Grandparent Program has
        been used in a prison in Ionia, Michigan to work with young offenders.
        The results are seen as important for both the offender and the
        volunteer.

259.   Kalab, Kathleen A. (1986, Sept-Oct). University teachers in senior
        community agencies. Educational Gerontology, 12, 441-451.

        Using herself as an example--a sociologist and a volunteer in a Foster
        Grandparent Program--the author of this article encourages university
        teachers to volunteer their skills and knowledge to agencies that work
        with older persons.

260.   Levy, Lorraine P. (1982). The integration of the Foster Grandparent
        Program with an acute care psychiatric service. Social Work in Health
        Care, 8(1), 27-35.

        The problems encountered in the development of a Foster Grandparent
        Program in an acute child and adolescent psychiatry ward are outlined
        in this article. Three Foster Grandmothers were integrated into multi-
        disciplinary teams and supervised by social workers.   The older
        volunteers showed that they could be useful to the team and produced
        a significant emotional exchange with the patients.

261.   Litigation Support Services. (1984, September). Impact evaluation of
        the Foster Grandparent Program on the foster grandparents: Final
        report (Contract No. 82-043-1018).   Washington, DC: ACTION
        Evaluation Division.

        This final report outlines the findings of a three-year longitudinal
        evaluation of the Foster Grandparent Program. The data show that for
        the volunteer participants, their overall functioning, mental health and
        social resources were maintained or improved over time.

262.   McCord, William T. (1982). "Giving them love": A study of foster
        grandparents at institutions and community schools. (Doctoral disserta-
        tion, Syracuse University, 1981). Dissertation Abstracts International,
        43, 140A.

        This is a qualitative study of the Foster Grandparent Program which
        examined the volunteers' own perceptions of their duties and work
        situations. The findings show that perspectives and duties both vary
        widely by volunteer setting. Some volunteers seemed to use their role
        to cope with their own pressing personal needs.

263.   McCord, William T. (1983, Summer). The pressure to conform: A
        study of Foster Grandparents at a state institution. Human Organiza-
        tion, 42, 162-166.

        Using unstructured interviews to collect information on the role of
        Foster Grandparents in an institution where 100 of the resident children
        have Foster Grandparents, the author highlights the difficult role the
        volunteers have fitting into an authoritarian and bureaucratic system
        where they are seen as a threat, disruptive, and not following day-to-
        day rules.

264.   Newman, Sally. (1989). A history of intergenerational programs,
        Journal of Children in Contemporary Society, 20(3-4), 1-16.

        This article is a chronology of significant events and initiatives that
        have contributed to the growth of intergenerational programs starting
        in 1963 with the Foster Grandparent Program and the Adopt a
        Grandparent Program. The thirty-one programs and events are each
        reviewed in short paragraphs. Seven state programs and initiatives are
        also discussed.

265.   Rhodes, Kent B. (1990). An analysis of constructs of extra-familial
        intergenerational relationships. (Doctoral dissertation, Peperdine
        University, 1990). Dissertation Abstracts International, 51, 3189B.

        This evaluative study of constructs of extra-familial intergenerational
        relationships between adolescents (ages 12-21) and elderly (ages 65 and
        older) participants in a Foster Grandparent Program, reports satisfacto-
        ry accomplishments of the following objectives: 1) to identify the
        elements of extra-familial intergenerational relationships within the
        existing literature while providing a report of the "state of the art" of
        such literature and 2) to establish and utilize a new, valid instrument
        for use in the evaluation of constructs and characteristics of extra-
        familial intergenerational relationships. Subjects reported the experi-
        ence as positive.

266.   Rouse, John T. (1982). Life satisfaction of the elderly as volunteer
        social support providers. Dissertation Abstracts International, 43,
        1305B.

        This study found no significant difference in life satisfaction between
        65 volunteers, actively involved in either the Foster Grandparent
        Program or the Senior Companionship Program, and 48 non-volunteers
        who were on the waiting lists of both programs. Findings did reveal,
        however, significant correlations between health, age, and number of
        hours per week volunteered and life satisfaction. These three variables
        were likewise found to be the best predictors of life satisfaction. In
        addition, clinical interviews were utilized among selected high and low
        scorers on the Life Satisfaction Index Z with the purpose of improving
        the quality of measurement of this variable.

267.   Sklar, Ellen, & Carlson, Cathy M. (1987). Foster Grandparents go
        inside prison walls. Aging, 365, 20-23.

This two-part article reviews   1) the experiences of four Foster Grandparents who volunteered to spend 20 hours a week working with inmates of a correctional institution in Vermont, and 2) the types of activities carried out by 74 volunteers in a large correctional facility in Whittier, California.

268.   Walls, Nancy. (1987). Three generations of love. <u>Aging</u>, <u>355</u>, 2-5.

Bringing together the Foster Grandparent Program with the Teenage Parent Alternative School Program (TPASP) in a suburb of Detroit, is the focus of this article which discusses student eligibility and the ways in which the older volunteers work in the child-care center of the program.

269.   Zalba, J., & McVeigh, J. (1982).   The marriage of research and service: The Foster Grandparent Program evaluation in the state of Michigan. <u>The Gerontologist</u>, <u>22</u>(5), 87-88.

This paper outlines the results of a two year study on program effectiveness from the perspective of the clients (the elderly) of 16 different Foster Grandparent Programs (N=1900). Results showed a high level of satisfaction with the program (93 percent).

270.   Ziegler, Suzzane, & Kind, Johanna. (1982). See entry number 231.

RSVP

271.   Arrella, Lorinda R. (1984). The Green County RSVP: A case study. Journal of Voluntary Action Research, 13,(3), 53-64.

This research was initiated as an evaluation of an RSVP program, intended to measure the success of volunteer projects. The data shows the demographics of the four groups used: inactive non-RSVP, inactive RSVP, active non-RSVP, and active RSVP. Data is also presented which shows the specific areas in which the organization was failing or succeeding.

272.   Booz-Allen and Hamilton, Inc. (1985, February). National Retired Senior Volunteer Program Participant Impact Evaluation: Round two report. Washington, DC: ACTION, Office of Policy and Planning/Evaluation Division.

This is an interim report on an assessment study concerning the impact of the national RSVP program using two of the three years of data. Information given includes: demographics, levels of functioning, psychological and sociological adjustment, and assessment of benefits. (See also entry number 273 for final report).

273.   Booz-Allen and Hamilton, Inc. (1985, September). National Retired Senior Volunteer Program participant impact evaluation: Final report. Washington, DC: ACTION, Office of Compliance/Evaluation Division. (ERIC Document Reproduction Service No. ED 265 388).

To assess impact of the national RSVP program over time, data were collected at three points: 1983, 1984, and 1985 looking at both veteran and new volunteers. The major findings describe the RSVP volunteer, their functional capabilities as related to length of service, and the effects of volunteerism on well being and outlook on live. The study recommends that program effectiveness may be increased by working to reduce first year attrition. (See also entry number 272 for interim report).

274.   Broadbent, JoAnne D. (1986). See entry number 162.

275.   Burrill, LaLee Orriss. (1987). The relationships among life satisfaction, volunteer job satisfaction, and volunteer hours in a Retired Senior Volunteer Program. Unpublished master's thesis, Central Washington University, Ellensburg.

This thesis looks at a sample (N = 104) of volunteers in an RSVP program to examine the relationships between life satisfaction, job satisfaction and number of hours spent in the volunteer role. The results do not show a significant relationship between volunteer satisfaction and volunteer hours.

276.   Ebnet, Jean Januschka, Dugan, Willis, Emslander, Sue, & Stone, Michelle. (1989, December). Self-perceptions of Retired Senior Volunteer Program Members: Annual RSVP evaluation report. St. Cloud, MN: Greater St. Cloud Retired Senior Volunteer Program. (ERIC Document Reproduction Service No. ED 316 668)

Three hundred and twenty-eight RSVP volunteers were used to evaluate the impact of volunteering on their lives, attitudes and adjustment. The data shows high levels of satisfaction, an increase in self-worth, an increase in their circle of friends, and help in meeting new friends.

277.   Fischer, K., Rapkin, B. D., & Rappaport, J. (1991). Gender and work history in the placement and perceptions of elder community volunteers. Psychology of Women Quarterly, 15(2), 261.

278.   Helping kids: The ripple effect (1987). See entry number 175.

This short review of an RSVP program in Monroe, Michigan describes how a small program has grown to a staff of 30 tutors who work with 90 children in 5 schools.

279.   Lewin, Martin. (1988, Summer). Library volunteers, a growing phenomenon. The Bookmark, 47(4), 249-251.

This article highlights at the many ways that volunteers can be used in a public library system. The assignment and recruitment of volunteers are outlined--demonstrating that a growing number of elderly volunteers are coming from RSVP programs.

280.   Morris-Gutierrez, Ellen, & Overs, Robert P. (1985). Retired Senior Volunteer Program of Waukesha County. Sussex, WI: Signpost.

Data from 213 volunteers (a 57% response rate) forms the basis of this evaluation of the RSVP program in Waukesha County, Wisconsin. Focus is on: the demographic characteristics of volunteers, services performed, and level of volunteer satisfaction.

281.   Nursing home residents join RSVP. (1981, Jan-Feb). See entry
        number 222.

282.   RSVP brings volunteering to nursing homes. (1982, Jan-Feb). See
        entry number 225.

283.   Sugarman, James H. (1982, October). RSVP in New York City: A
        study of volunteer impact and opportunity [Special issue]. The
        Gerontologist, 22, 208. Abstract of paper presented at the 35th annual
        meeting of The Gerontological Society of America.

        As part of an evaluation study, a survey of 177 out of 8000 RSVP
        members in New York City shows that the need for volunteer
        opportunities grows as people get older and that the impact of the
        volunteer service by the aged helps both the volunteers and the
        communities they serve. Seventy-five percent of the volunteers felt
        they were making an impact and over ninety percent felt a great deal
        of satisfaction with their role.

284.   Yuknavage, Pat. (1982, May-June). Intergenerational issues. Aging,
        327-328, 15-19.

        This general review article discusses the many types of programs
        coming out of ACTION and RSVP. Examples used are: work with
        youthful offenders, handicapped youngsters and the old-old, lifetime
        learning, and death and dying programs.

Peace Corps

285.   American Association for International Aging. (1987, April). Strategy
        guide for working with senior Americans. Peace Corps, unpublished
        document.

        The use, since 1984, of senior volunteers in the Peace Corps led to this
        publication in which sections are given to first; describing trends in
        aging in America, second; the progress of the Peace Corp's use of
        older volunteers, third; the concerns and issues which have arisen--both
        from the volunteer and staff perspectives--and fourth; a set of recom-
        mendations and strategies to address those concerns.

286.   Brooks, Mila Williams. (1988, January). Special report on seniors in
        Peace Corps. Peace Corps, unpublished document.

        That senior Peace Corps volunteers feel overseas staff are insensitive
        to their needs and learning styles is the focus of this short paper.
        Based on experience as Country Director in the Dominican Republic,
        the author outlines actions to improve training, increase coordination,
        review early terminations and implement special language training for
        the older volunteer.

287.   Hurley, Dan. (1985, July). Call to care. 50 Plus, 25(7), 42-45.

        This essay reviews the ways in which older volunteers are used in
        VISTA and the Peace Corps.

288.   Murphy, Caryle. (1988, May). Peace Corps wants you! Fifty Plus,
        28(5), 26-29.

        A review and various case studies of the older volunteer, as part of the
        Peace Corps, comprise the central theme of this essay.

289.   Peace Corps (U.S.). (1984, November). Older volunteer study. Peace
        Corps, unpublished document.

        A collection of reports on the use of older volunteers in the Peace
        Corps makes up the bulk of this publication. These reports are
        reviewed and a set of recommendations made as well as directions
        given to the agency to increase the awareness of the use of the older
        volunteer and to continue to collect information to compare the older
        volunteer with other volunteers.

290.   Rymph, David. (1984). A profile of older volunteers, 1979-1984.
       Peace Corps, unpublished document.

       The peace corps is the focus of this monograph which outlines the
       characteristics of 742 older volunteers. Twelve key findings are
       outlined, based on the data which are then presented in table form.

291.   Sykes, William. (1981, Summer). Retirees in the Peace Corps: New
       careers with respect. Generations, 5(4), 32-34.

       Retirees who have entered the Peace Corps are the focus of this article.
       The author points out that there is no upper limit and that there are
       financial benefits available covering a modest living allowance,
       readjustment allowance, and travel.

292.   Udall, Patricia. (1990, January). Seniors and Peace Corps: A summary
       report with recommendations. Peace Corps, unpublished document.

       A review of the use of volunteers from 1963 to 1988 is made,
       followed by statistics based on 1988 data. A short review of ten major
       studies carried out over a seven year period (1981-1988) is then
       presented. This report shows that few recommendations have been
       implemented out of the 114 proposed and therefore, focuses on five
       major recommendations that should be carried out in the 1990's.

Chapter 6
General Models and Programs

293.   American Association of Homes for the Aging. (1985). <u>The volunteer leader: Essays on the role of trustees of non-profit facilities and services for the aging</u>. Washington, DC: Author.

The American Association of Homes for the Aging produced this publication in order to provide information for new volunteer board members. The topics covered--the board and its organization, organizing a board, the relationship of a board to the administrator of a home, and the major functions of a board--are well described so that they can be used to evaluate performance and identify areas for additional attention.

294.   American Association of Retired Persons. (1984). <u>Community programs idea book</u>. Washington, DC: Author.

In order to help communities become involved in using older volunteers in community projects, this publication outlines over twenty program topics that have a history of success. Such topics range from Hospice to telephone reassurance. Also included are ways to select the best program for a given community. This is a very useful publication as an introduction to the range of programs that are available for replication.

295. American Association of Retired Persons. (1988). A resource guide for incorporating older volunteers into parent aide programs. Washington, DC: Author.

This useful monograph is a review of a project to promote and enhance strategies to prevent child abuse by developing linkages between child welfare and aging networks. The project was piloted in five sites across the United States. This publication gives the basic process used and includes the working documents--establishing a task force, recruiting older volunteers, involving the networks--and bibliographic material.

296. American Bar Association. (1987, September). Pro bono seniorum: Volunteer lawyers projects for the elderly. Chicago, IL: Author.

A 1987 survey by the American Bar Association Commission on Legal Problems identified forty-one programs in 26 states, and the results describe these programs. Planners of such pro bono projects will find this information useful as well as the "ten tenets" suggested to aid in designing new programs.

297. Beaver, Linda Zane, & Lidoff, Lorraine. (1983). Program innovations in aging: Vol 1. Stimulating the development of older volunteer programs. Washington, DC: National Council on the Aging.

A guide for putting volunteer programs into place in areas that lack extensive service resources is outlined in this publication. Covered are the topics of who should use the model, where the model can be best adapted, and how it can be implemented. This is one of the few models that has been based on rural experiences.

298. Beaver, Linda Zane, & Lidoff, Lorraine. (1983). Stimulating the development of older volunteer programs (Vol I). Washington, DC: National Council on the Aging.

The purpose of this volume is to act as a guide to provide the impetus and expertise to help volunteer programs develop in local communities rather than how to run volunteer programs. The model to be used is outlined with emphasis on how to put the model in place, the resources needed--including such topics as planning, public relations, fund raising and grantsmanship--and evaluation strategies.

299. Bell, William G. (1982, October). Volunteers in community transport for the elderly in the United Kingdom: Lessons for the United States

[Special issue]. The Gerontologist, 22, 207-208. Abstract of paper presented at the 35th annual meeting of The Gerontological Society of America.

Findings from on-site surveys of a sample of transportation systems in the U.K. are used in this paper to suggest some new directions that may be tried in the U.S. In order to increase the supply of volunteers, it is suggested that programs turn to new sources of supply, redefine the tasks of paid staff to accommodate the skill levels of the volunteers, and provide insurance protection.

300.   Blum, Barbara B. (1984). Helping teenage mothers. Public Welfare, 42(1), 17-21.

Project Redirection is a program in which each teen is assigned to an older female volunteer who acts as a role model and who helps locate and use services (e.g., register for school, meet clinic appointments or arrange child care). The success rates in this program are outlined relative to school retention, job participation and reduction in new pregnancies. The artile describes the original sites and outlines where replications are being carried out.

301.   Bock, Kathy (Ed.). (1990). See entry number 233.

302.   Bruer, Ruth A. (1986, April). A hands-on guide to volunteer development. Available from: Center for Volunteer Development, CEC-CVD Suite, Virginia Tech, Blacksburg, VA 24061-0150 ($10.00).

This is a self-study guide that was based on a survey of 215 organizations in Virginia and consists of four self-study packages designed to help directors of volunteers strengthen programs serving older people. The four separate chapters cover the topics of: Why have volunteers and who directs them?, job descriptions, recruitment and placement, management and supervision, and staff/volunteer relations.

303.   Buckley, Susan. (1985). Parent aides provide support to high risk families. Children Today, 14(5), 16-19.

A review of the program: Parent Aide Support Service (PASS) in Lincoln, Nebraska, is contained in this article which discusses the ways in which volunteers can provide nurturance, acceptance, and support for high-risk families.

304.   Campbell, Ruth, & Chenoweth, Barbara. (1981). Peer supports for
        older adults. Ann Arbor, MI: University of Michigan, Turner
        Geriatric Clinic.

        This manual describes a model in which elderly volunteer peer
        counselors provide education and counseling to older adults. Descrip-
        tion of the model is followed by discussions of: 1) the relationship
        between physical and mental health, 2) an overview of the peer support
        network, 3) training, recruitment and responsibilities of the volunteers,
        4) workshops, 5) the effects of the program, and 6) evaluation instru-
        ments.

305.   Coughlin, Teresa A., & Meiners, Mark R. (1990). Service Credit
        Banking: Issues in program development. Journal of Aging and Social
        Policy, 2(2), 25-41.

        A review of programs that allow volunteers to earn credits, later
        reedemable for comparable services when they may require them, is the
        major focus of this article. Topics covered are: target beneficiaries,
        participants ages, credit guarantees, credit flow, program structures and
        sponsorship, and types and levels of services.

306.   Essex, Virginia. (1987). Building corporate/voluntary partnerships for
        and by older persons: A resource to assist aging network providers.
        Miami: Southeast Florida Center on Aging.

        A resource booklet designed for persons who are charged with
        implementing volunteer services has as its focus the growing relation-
        ship between the corporate and voluntary sectors. The major topics
        covered are: recruitment, corporate programs in action, corporate
        volunteer councils (coalitions), management issues, and how linkages
        are made.

307.   Farkas, Kathleen J., & Milligan, Sharon E. (1991, Nov-Dec). Family
        Friends evaluation: Volunteers tell of benefits from service to others.
        Perspective on Aging, 20(6), 26-29.

        In this article, data from a 1989 evaluation of the--at that time--eight
        existing Family Friends programs is summarized with a focus upon
        demographics and perceptions of the volunteers. The program, which
        trains and matches volunteers over age 55 with families of children
        with disabilities, is predominantly perceived by the volunteers as
        providing an opportunity to: work with children, help others, replace
        or fufill social roles, and/or acquire/apply new skills. High levels of

satisfaction with the training and operation of the program were reported by the volunteers, as was the beneficial and rewarding nature of their roles as Family Friends.

308.   Frankle, Helene, & Gordon, Virginia K. (1983). Helping Selma: A report on a therapist-volunteer relationship. Social Casework, 64, 291-299.

A single case study is used to explore, over a ten year period, the relationship between a social worker and an older volunteer with an elderly widow. Separate narratives by both the social worker and the volunteer outlined the reasons for the widow's depression and the gradual improvement over time.

309.   Greenblatt, Sadell T. (1990, February). Expansion research project: June '87-August '87. In Little Brothers Friends of the Elderly. Report on National Expansion Research Plan for FY90 expansion sites. Chicago: Little Brothers Friends of the Elderly.

This is an evaluation report of data collected from just over 400 volunteers--a third of which are over the age of 65--who, through the Little Brothers program, provide short-term, comprehensive social services and referral and long-term emotional support to lonely and isolated elderly. The general findings of the research are outlined and a set of criterea are used to allow the agency to select possible future sites for their program.

310.   Harnett, Joan. (1989, May-June). An intergenerational support system for child welfare families. Child Welfare, 68(3), 347-353.

The Intergenerational Support System (ISS) is described, looking at the program's origins, recruitment, training, and evaluative procedures. Senior volunteers served as support persons for families with problems, young parents and single mothers. The average length of contact was six months, but breaking the relationship in order to move to a new case created conflict for the volunteers.

311.   Hendricks, Jon. (1988). Preparing and utilizing older volunteers to provide in-service gerontology training. Washington, DC: U.S. Department of Health and Human Services.

This innovative Gerontology Extension Program demonstration project trained forty retired volunteers to function for a six month period as in-service trainers at agency sites in Kentucky. The evaluation suggests that the volunteers could learn new materials, enhance their own self-worth and deliver training which is perceived as useful by agency and program personnel. The training focused on: 1) home health care, 2) consumer economics, 3) drug and medication regimes, 4) nutrition and food preparation and 5) coping and adaptation skills. Recommendations are given as to how to duplicate the success of the program.

312.   Hillman, Deborah J. (1988). Friends in need: An ethnographic portrait of a senior volunteer friendly-visiting program. Dissertation Abstracts International, 48, 2916A.

This study is an examination of Project Assist (Active Seniors and Isolated Seniors Together) in which older volunteer caregivers provided supplemental services and companionship. Examined were the programs effect on staff, host agencies, volunteers, clients and the community. The data indicate that the emotional and social needs of both the clients and volunteers were served.

313.   Hoffman, Stephanie B. (1983). Peer counselor training with the elderly. The Gerontologist, 23, 358-360.

An historical account of peer counselor training with the elderly is outlined. Suggestions on advertising, screening, program formant, and the development of practicum placement are covered. The role and helpfulness of the older peer counselor are examined as well.

314.   Hood, Thomas, & Geis, Linda. (1982, April). The volunteer transportation program: Some suggestions and cautions in the use of volunteers as drivers, escorts, and other transportation workers. Knoxville: University of Tennessee. (NTIS No. PB82-238064)

This manual is intended to serve as an aide to social service agencies, voluntary associations and churches utilizing voluntary transportation services. These services are provided, as briefly discussed, increasingly by senior citizens. Topics covered include: 1) reasons for utilizing a volunteer transportation program, 2) characteristics/problems, 3) organization of programs, and 4) resources.

315.   Independent Transportation Management Services, Inc. (1990). Liability insurance and the volunteer driver: An analysis of the impact of insurance availability and cost on Minnesota volunteer drivers and volunteer transportation programs. Minneapolis, MN: Minnesota Department of Transportation.

Eighty-four percent of the volunteer drivers surveyed for this analysis were age fifty-five or older, many of whom feared losing their driver's license and thus their independence should they be liable in the event of an accident. This publication offers much insight in terms of liability issues as related to older volunteer drivers.

316.   Korte, Charles, & Gupta, Vasudha. (1991). A program of friendly visitors as network builders. The Gerontologist, 31, 404-407.

In order to strengthen the social support networks of the isolated, elderly volunteers were trained as visitors and matched with individuals who showed serious levels of social isolation. The volunteers were trained either as network-builders or friendly visitors and the six month evaluation showed little difference in the amount of contact either group had with the clients' network.

317.   McCurley, Steve, & Lynch, Rick. (1989). Essential volunteer management. Downers Grove, IL: The Volunteer Mangement Series of V M Systems.

As a companion piece to the book 101 Ideas for Volunteer Programs, (number 319) this work has as its focus, management of programs. The subjects of planning, creating jobs, recruitment, screening and interviewing, training, supervising and retention are very throughly covered as are volunteer-staff relations.

318.   McCurley, Steve, & Vineyard, Sue. (1988). 101 tips for volunteer recruitment. Downers Grove, IL: Heritage Arts.

Recruitment is the major subject covered with emphasis on planning, the actual process, and comparisons between mass and targeted recruitment. Special attention is given to: board recruitment and how to get the correct people into committee positions, as well as general membership recruitment.

319.   McCurley, Steve, & Vineyard, Sue. (1986). 101 ideas for volunteer programs. Downers Grove, IL: Heritage Arts.

This is another monograph in a series dealing with volunteering with many suggestions outlined in the form of questions or actions covering such areas as planning, recruitment, screening, training, supervising, marketing and volunteer/staff relations.

320.   Miller, Meridith, Ross, Lorraine, & Beall, George Thomas. (1984).
        Voluntarism in action for the aging: A handbook for national voluntary
        organization initiatives in aging. Washington, DC: National Council
        on the Aging.

        To encourage and assist national voluntary organizations to develop
        programs on behalf of the elderly, this publication looks at the
        opportunities and difficulties in initiating such new programs. Based
        on the experiences from Project VIAA (Voluntarism in Action for
        Aging) the handbook examines examples of age-related projects, offers
        tips on replicating such projects, and summarizes key project findings.

321.   Mills, Ann K. (1990). Neighbor helping neighbor: Developing a
        volunteer service network. Rochester, VT: The Village Computery.

        Community Care as a rural program was developed over a five year
        perild in Vermont and this handbook is a review of the program with
        the necessary suggestions for those who wish to replicate it. Covered
        in the guide are: getting started, insurance, budgets, funding,
        recruiting, training, locating need, evaluation and follow-up, and
        recognition. Good illustrations and forms are included.

322.   Morrow-Howell, Nancy, & Ozawa, Martha N. (1987). Helping
        network: Seniors to seniors. The Gerontologist, 27, 17-20.

        A description of the program System to Assure Elderly Services
        (STAES) is described so that other communities can duplicate the
        model. Elderly volunteers are trained to perform two major functions:
        instrumental support (e.g., telephone reassurance, socializing or
        shopping) and referrals to service agencies, as needed.

323.   Morrow-Howell, Nancy. (1989, November). The service credit
        exchange: Service insurance for older adults. Paper presented at the
        42nd annual scientific meeting of the Gerontological Society of
        America, Minneapolis, MN.

        This paper, as part of a symposium on the use of volunteers in health
        and human service settings, looks at the Service Credit Exchange
        Program. The objective of this program is to provide service insurance
        for older adults.

324.   Netting, F. Ellen, & Hinds, Howard N. (1984). Volunteer advocates
        in long term care: Local implementation of a federal mandate. The
        Gerontologist, 24, 13-15.

The purpose of this article is to describe the volunteer advocacy program developed by the East Tennessee Advocacy Assistance Program set up to assist the ombudsman/director in resolving problems and complaints made by residents in long-term care facilities. The authors recommend that effective participation by volunteers requires intensive training, well-defined policies and procedures, coordination, and adequate supervision.

325.   Newman, Sally, & Bocian, Kathleen. (1986, August). Connecting the Generations. Ageing International, 13(3), 13-15.

Established in 1978, Generations Together, a part of the University of Pittsburgh Center for Social and Urban Research, is an agency responsible for the pioneering of several successful intergenerational programs involving, as of 1986, the participation of over 20,000 youths and 1,500 elderly. Examples of the types of programs implemented, shared components of the programs, as well as an example of one program evaluation, are presented in this brief but very informative article.

326.   Ozawa, Martha N., & Morrow-Howell, Nancy. (in press). Service utilization by the well-organized elderly. Journal of Aging and Human Development.

To be able to continue a government based case management service program--after the project had to be terminated because of the lack of federal funding--the program used healthy volunteers trained to "look after" the needs of frail elders. Over 100 well-informed volunteers were trained and this research looks at the degree and types of service utilization.

327.   Petty, Beryl J., & Cusack, Sandra A. (1989). Assessing the impact of a seniors' peer counseling program. Educational Gerontology, 15(49), 49-64.

The seniors' peer counseling program at Century House in New Westminster, British Columbia is the subject of this article which focuses upon training strategies and principles for senior counselors, as opposed to content. Evaluation of an 18-month training program for senior counselors (N=18) produced generally favorable results.

328.   Pilsuk, Marc, & Minkler, Meredith. (1980). Supportive networks: Life ties for the elderly. Journal of Social Issues, 36(2), 95-116.

Six different programs are examined and used to illustrate the growth in importance of social support networks, either in public service settings or in voluntary associations as needs are transferred from the family. In several of the programs, the role of the older volunteer is outlined or alluded to. The programs reviewed deal with the Chinese, Japanese and inner city residents of San Francisco, a self-help group in Berkeley, a Senior Gleaners program which collects and distributes surplus food, and the local chapters of the Grey Panthers.

329.   Poser, Ernest G., & Engles, Mary Louise. (1983).   Self-efficacy assessment and peer group assistance in a preretirement intervention. Educational Gerontology, 9, 159-169.

The use of peer volunteer counselors to lead a weekend intervention dealing with retirement transition is the subject of this study. The control verses experimental group comparisons indicates a main effect after a three month follow-up on the variables of self-efficacy, retirement knowledge and retirement morale.

330.   Pynoos, J., Hade-Kaplan, B., & Fleisher, D. (1984).   Intergenerational neighborhood networks: A basis for aiding the frail elderly. The Gerontologist, 24, 233-37.

Living Independently through Neighborhood Cooperation (LINK) is a project that was built in order to organize a community to provide mutual help to its members, with special emphasis on the frail elderly. The elderly served both as volunteers and as recipients with the program demonstrating that the frail elderly were provided with more services, acted as volunteers, increased their life satisfaction and participated in more social activities. The program is multifaceted and described in some detail.

331.   Reece, Carolyn. (1988, Jan-Feb).   Older volunteers and youths with disabilities team up to find jobs. Children Today, 17(1), 14-15.

This article reviews Team Work Intergenerational Project, a program in which older volunteers are used to teach job skills to youths with learning disabilities, physical impairments, or sensory limitations prior to their entering the workforce.

332.   Report of research findings: Chicago Senior Citizens Self Help Project. (1980). Chicago: Office for Senior Citizens and Handicapped.

This report covers the history and evaluation of a model of an informal support network which used existing senior citizen groups or clubs to expand, create, promote and link these groups. The objective of the project was to increase the use of the informal support network by the elderly community. A non-random sample of 47 clubs/groups was used and evaluated. Both the successful changes found, as well as the evaluation instruments used, are outlined.

333.   Retirement village volunteers set up programs for residents. (1981, Jan-Feb). Aging, 315-316, 41-42.

A Dial-A-Ride service, started and operated by older volunteers in a New Jersey retirement community, is reviewed in this article which outlines the costs involved in the services, the types of vehicles used, and the scope of the taxi service in particular.

334.   Sachs, Martha. (1983, March-April). Housing CSI-a successful senior housing cooperative. Aging, 337, 14-18.

This detailed article looks at a unique feature of a consumer cooperative that manages housing for low to moderate income elderly--using resident volunteers to manage the various complexes.

335.   Seguin, Mary M., & McConney, Polly F. (1983, Spring). Older volunteers and new frontiers. The Journal of Volunteer Administration, 1(3), 50-57.

This article presents data on how 103 volunteers were used by the Gerontological Center at the Andrus Foundation. The types of jobs done are reviewed as well as the characteristics of the volunteers. Also included is the organizational consideration needed to use and build a volunteer staff.

336.   Seguin, Mary M. (1984). Social work practice with senior adult volunteers in organizations run by paid personnel. In Florence S. Schwartz (Ed.). Voluntarism and social work practice: A growing collaboration. Lanham, MD: University Press.

This paper reviews the characteristics of 64 volunteers who worked in the Andrus Gerontological Center and is followed by a review of the principles for practice that guided both volunteers and the paid staff. The review of the guidelines and how to apply them to other settings is discussed.

337. Shine, Marsha S., & Steitz, Jean A. (1989, Summer). Retirement
      housing resident volunteer programs. The Journal of Volunteer
      Administration, 7(4), 1-3.

      This short article describes a resident volunteer program showing that
      such a program can offer residents: the opportunity for active
      participation, meaningful decision-making, and increased involvement.
      In this study of a high-rise residence, over 62 percent of the 107
      residents were involved to some extent in the volunteer program.
      Challenges, problems and benefits are outlined.

338. Sorenson, Gloria. (1981). Older persons and service providers: An
      instructor's training guide. New York: Human Sciences Press.

      Directed toward instructors of persons working with the elderly, this
      training book looks at general awareness of aging issues, physiological
      changes, sexuality, intimacy, listening skills, and various therapies
      (e.g., music, pet). This is a publication that would be usefully
      employed in the training of older volunteers.

339. Steinman, S. (1987). Comparing the impact of a peer reception
      program with a traditional method of welcoming newcomers to the
      senior center. Dissertation Abstracts International, 48, 1520A.

      A peer reception program was evaluated to see what impact it had on
      welcoming newcomers to a senior center. Peer volunteers oriented
      newcomers during their first day at the center and compared with a
      randomly selected control group, the treatment group showed signifi-
      cantly higher scores on all outcome measures: frequency of contact
      with center, quality of contact, attitude toward center and life-satisfac-
      tion.

340. Stunkel, Edith (Ed.). (1989). Volunteers in motion: A guide for
      successful volunteerism. Manhattan: Kansas State University, Center
      for Aging.

      A short but useful guide to agencies using older volunteers, this
      publication contains some of the necessary steps to be taken in terms
      of: job descriptions, rights and responsibilities, evaluation, confidenti-
      ality, and 99 ways to recognize volunteers. Included also is a short
      bibliography, as well as information on other resource organizations.

341.   Struntz, Karen A., & Reville, Shari (Eds.). (1985). Growing together: An intergenerational sourcebook. Washington, DC: American Association of Retired Persons.

This is a very useful compendium of intergenerational programs in which an array of contributors outline successful models of generic programs that have been widely duplicated. The volume also includes a listing of national organizations that have intergenerational programs, and a short annotated bibliography.

342.   Tice, Carol. (1982, May-June). Creating caring communities: Linking the generations. Aging, 327-328, 20-23.

Teaching-Learning Communities (TL-C), a program started in Ann Arbor, Michigan, is reviewed in this article. This intergenerational program is outlined in detail and other types of programs discussed.

343.   Ventura-Merkel, Catherine, & Newman, Patricia (Eds.). (1983). Voluntary action and older Americans: A catalogue of program profiles. Washington, DC: National Council on the Aging.

344.   Vineyard, Sue. (1984). Marketing magic for volunteer programs. Downers Grove, IL: Heritage Arts.

Although the older volunteer is not the focus of this book, its useful-ness covers the recruitment and retention of all volunteers. Emphasis is on the concept of marketing and the publication leads the reader through the necessary steps (with exercises) from assessment, recruit-ment and getting the correct publicity for a given program.

345.   Vionkur-Kaplan, D., Cibulski, O., Spero, S., & Bergman, S. (1982). Oldster to oldster: An example of mutual aid through friendly visiting among Israeli elderly. Journal of Gerontological Social Work, 4(1), 75-91.

346.   Warrick, Pamela. (1986). Older volunteers: A valuable resource. Washington DC: American Association of Retired Persons.

A very brief intoduction to the main tasks that are needed to put together a volunteer program using the older person is outlined. Covered in this booklet are: job descriptions, recruiting, training, evaluation, placement, insurance, and confidentiality. Several resources are outlined at the end of the publication.

347.   Whitehead, Minnie M., & Nokes, Kathleen M. (1990). An examina-
         tion of demographic variables, nurturance, and empathy among
         homosexual and heterosexual Big Brother/Big Sister volunteers.
         Journal of Homosexuality, 19(4), 89-101.

         In this exploratory study, a sixty-one percent response rate (N=219) to
         a questionnaire sent to all volunteers in the Big Brother/Big Sister
         program in San Francisco indicates that there was no significant
         difference in demographics, nuturance scores, or empathy scores based
         on sexual orientation.   Any gender differences were found to be
         consistent with earlier studies.

Chapter 7
Special Populations

Widows and Widowers

348.   Parham, Iris, Romaniuk, Michael, Priddy, Michael, & Wenzel, Charlotte. (1980, May-June). Widowhood peer counseling. Aging, 307-308, 42-46.

Following a review of the peer counseling concept, this article looks at programs that have used older volunteers as peer counselors and focuses on a program started at Virginia Commonwealth University.

349.   Vachon, M. L. S., Lyall, W. A. L., Rogers, J., Freedman-Letofsky, K., & Freeman, S. J. J. (1980, November). A controlled study of self-help intervention for widows. American Journal of Psychiatry, 137, 1380-1384.

A two year study of 162 widows in Toronto paired 68 with a widow contact who had participated in a training seminar which examined problems of bereavement, support counseling, and the spectrum of community resources. The findings, when compared with the control group of 94 widows, shows that the differences at the follow-up times of 1, 6, 12 and 24 months indicate that those receiving counseling followed the same general course of adaptations, but at an accelerated rate.

Developmentally Disabled/Visually Impaired

350.   Amaral, Phyllis L., Ringering, LaDonna S., & Genensky, Samual W. (1985, April). Older partially sighted volunteers: Advocates and community counselors in a rehabilitation program for the visually impaired. Santa Monica, CA: The Center for Partially Sighted. (NTIS No. SHR 0013521 XAB)

This study examines the effects of using partially sighted older adults to counsel visually impaired elderly using both a Speaker's Bureau and follow-up weekly peer telephone calls. Through 97 presentations and over 50 follow-up telephone calls, the research shows that calls resulted in a significant increase in activity level and understanding of the vision condition. In addition, there appeared to be an increased sense of accomplishment and productivity on the part of the peer counselors.

351.   Berkman, Susan C. (1984). Community service by visually impaired older adults. Journal of Visual Impairment and Blindness, 78, 10-12.

The Community Outreach Program, run by the Braille Institute, is reviewed in this short article with a focus on the training and placement of older blind persons in various volunteer positions. Major outcomes were the increasing self-confidence of the volunteers and teaching local agencies more about blindness and the capabilities of blind workers.

352.   Bernstein, Bebe. (1985, Spring). Growing with the Arts. Journal of Reading, Writing, and Learning Disabilities International, 1(3), 25-28.

In this very short article, the author outlines how the Retirement with Enrichment, the Arts and Purpose (REAP) program was married with a Very Special Arts Festival Program (VSAF) to provide a non-competitive atmosphere for disabled children, youth and adults in the completion of visual and performing arts.

353.   Creekmore, W. N., & Creekmore, N. N. (1983, Feb). Senior citizens as paraprofessionals in teaching severely handicapped children. The Exceptional Child, 49(5), 455-457.

354.   Del Green Associates, Inc. (1984). Use of volunteers in the transportation of elderly and handicapped persons: Final report. Washington DC: Office of Technical Assistance, Urban Mass Transportation Administration.

This report is a descriptive analysis of a review of thirteen volunteer transportation programs throughout the United States. Common characteristics of these programs and the transportation volunteer are presented. Descriptions of the individual programs are offered in addition to examples of the materials and forms used.

355.   Fengler, Alfred P., & Goodrich, Nancy. (1980).   Money isn't everything: Opportunities for elderly handicapped men in a sheltered workshop. The Gerontologist, 20, 636-641.

The use of the severely handicapped older person as a volunteer is explored in this article. The results show that the volunteer role was both meaningful and significant for this group of elderly with helping others, getting out of the house and sociability being the most important reasons for interest and participation in the program.

356.   Foster Grandparent transforms aged mental patient. (1980, Nov-Dec). Aging, 313-314, 40-41.

This short article outlines the history of how an older mental patient was able to become a Foster Grandparent to two mentally retarded children. The benefits to both generations are presented as well.

357.   Jones, Clare B. (1986, Fall).   Grandparents read to special pre-schoolers. Teaching Exceptional Children, 19, 36-37.

This article describes the year-long Grandparent Read to Me Project in which senior volunteers were recruited to read aloud to learning disabled 3 to 5 year-olds at a preschool for the learning disabled in Lakewood, Ohio. Positive results were reported on the program which included training sessions for both the volunteers and the children. This project received the 1985-86 "Best Intergenerational Showcase Award" from the American Association on Aging.

358.   Kultgen, Phyllis, Rinck, Christine, Calkins, Carl F., & Intagliata, James. (1986, April). Expanding the life chances and social support networks of elderly developmentally disabled persons. Kansas City, MO: UMKC Institute for Human Development. (NTIS No. SHR 0013992 XAB. 8704)

This report looks at a study in which older volunteers were assigned to sponsor individual seniors with developmental disabilities and introduce them into a senior center. In addition to these one-on-one friendships, the volunteers were encouraged to introduce their client, not only within the senior center, but into other aspects of community life as well. The study shows a high success and satisfaction rate for the client, the disabled elder, and the older volunteer.

359.   Kultgen, Phyllis. (1988). An instructor's guide to training volunteers: Companion programs for older persons with developmental disabilities and their non-disabled peers. Kansas City: University of Missouri-Kansas City, Institute for Human Development, Interdisciplinary Training Center on Gerontology and Developmental Disabilities.

This publication is a manual designed to assist program developers and planners to access and use companion volunteers, in various community settings, to help older persons with developmental disabilities. The topics covered are: recruitment, selection and choice of sites for volunteers, the mechanics of programs, and the content of volunteer training.

360.   Lyon, Philip E., Medved, Richard M., Burns, James, & Sarachan-Deily, Ann Beth. (1985, March). Preservice training of senior citizens as special education volunteers. Paper presented at the 5th National Rural Special Education Conference. Bellingham, WA. (ERIC Document Reproduction Service No. ED 261 833)

In this paper, the authors propose a three-year project designed to train senior citizens as volunteer aides in special education classrooms. Projected long-term outcomes include: 1) serving as a model for similar projects and 2) aiding school systems which serve handicapped children by creating a network of training systems and personnel.

361.   Reece, Carolyn. (1988, Jan-Feb). See entry number 331.

362.   Schmidt, Ann V. (1985). Family friends. Children Today, 14(5), 12-15.

The Family Friends Project, the focus of this article, is a project sponsored by NCOA in which older volunteers work with families who have either handicapped or chronically ill children. Many examples are provided and the expansion of the original Washington, DC program is discussed.

363.   Zimmer, Lawrence. (1988, Summer). Senior citizens help the visually and physically impaired. The Bookmark, 46(4), 242-244.

The New York State Library for the Blind and Visually Handicapped (LBVH) offers services in 55 upstate counties. RSVP volunteers were used in a pilot project to seek out potential users and help them to register for library services. These volunteers contacted the home-bound elderly, as well as those in nursing homes. Other organizations which utilize older volunteers are described as well.

Racial or Ethnic Minorities

364.   Allen, Katherine, & Chin-Sang, Victoria. (1990). A lifetime of work:
        The context and meanings of leisure for aging Black women. The
        Gerontologist, 30(6), 734-740.

        This qualitative study assumes a life course perspective in its examina-
        tion of work and leisure as interrelated contexts in the lives of 30
        African-American women, some of whom mentioned and/or described
        voluntary services they provide.

365.   Ashby, Vicki R. (1981). See entry number 256.

366.   Height, Dorothy I., Toya, James, Kamikawa, Louise, & Maldonado,
        David. (1981, Summer). See entry number 24.

367.   In reaching and serving Hispanic elderly, volunteers can make the
        difference: A resource book for program guidance. (1985). Washing-
        ton, DC: COSSMHO (The National Coalition of Hispanic Mental
        Health and Human Services Organizations.)

        This resource book is based on information gathered by the National
        Coalition of Hispanic Mental Health and Human Services Organizations
        to show how volunteers can be the crucial catalyst needed to overcome
        the barriers to helping the older Hispanic population which as a group
        are underrepresented in many existing programs. The findings are
        based on a national survey of 220 programs in 37 states. Recommen-
        dations are made on the promoting of and motivation of older volun-
        teers to aid the Hispanic elderly.

368.   Johnson, Colleen L., & Barer, Barbara M. (1990). Families and
        networks among older inner-city Blacks. The Gerontologist, 30(6),
        726-733.

        Although not dealing directly with volunteers, this article, which
        examines networks used by inner-city blacks, is of interest. For
        blacks, the use of extended kin networks and fictive kin, as well as the
        role of "church mother" could be used as indicators of volunteer
        activity.

369.   McCabe, Melvina L. (1988). Health care accessibility for the elderly
        on the Navajo reservation. Pride Institute Journal of Long-Term Health
        Care, 7(4), 22-26.

370. Maldonado, David, Jr., & Applewhite, Steven. (1986). The Hispanic elderly: Empowerment through training. Arlington: University of Texas, Center for Chicano Aged, graduate school of social work.

This is a manual specifically focused on the training of Chicano elderly to help each other. A review of the Hispanic elderly is followed by specific guidelines on how to manage and deliver training programs to older Hispanics, how to train older Hispanic volunteers, and how to involve elderly Hispanics in community participation. Information on training in life-coping skills is offered and a very useful bibliography on older Hispanics is provided as well.

371. Milligan, Sharon, Maryland, Patricia, Ziegler, Henry, & Ward, Anna. (1987). Natural helpers as street health workers among the black urban elderly. The Gerontologist, 27, 712-715.

The results of a 5 year experience in which volunteers--mostly elderly-- in a black urban community provided geriatric health outreach, are outlined in this article. This outreach program enhanced the service organizations and showed that volunteers can be recruited and trained to assist families in the monitoring of the well-being of frail elderly.

372. Morrow-Howell, Nancy, Lott, Leeanne, & Ozawa, Martha. (1990, September). The impact of race on volunteer helping relationships among the elderly. Social Work, 35, 395-402.

This is an important study which examines the influence of race in the relationships between volunteers and the people they serve in a community self-help program. Looking at the data collected from 83 volunteers (average age 65) it was found that race does not affect helping behavior as measured by time committed to service or satisfaction of clients. However, higher levels of contact and client satisfaction were reported among same-race dyads.

373. Pardo, Mary. (1990). Mexican American women grassroots community activists: Mothers of East Los Angeles. Frontiers, 11(1), 1-7.

374. Ross, Lorraine N., & Lidoff, Lorraine. (1984). Senior volunteer literacy tutors. Washington, DC: National Council on the Aging.

This handbook focuses on a model in which older volunteers are used to help non-English speaking community residents with conversational English. A step-by-step process is outlined dealing with the assembly of resources, implementation procedures, training, funding, resource materials (used or available) and sample forms.

375.   Stanford, E. P., & Tisdale, M. B. (1982). The minority retiree: An untapped resource. San Diego, CA: San Diego State University, University Center on Aging, College of Human Services.

With data collected from 600 Black, Hispanic and Anglo elderly in San Diego and Denver, this study found: 1) most organizations use elderly volunteers, 2) transportation was a major barrier to senior involvement, 3) compared to Anglos and Blacks, Latinos were more likely to do volunteer work, 4) among the non-volunteers, one-third would like to volunteer, and 5) poor health and other obligations were given as the most frequently cited barriers to volunteerism.

376.   Wentowski, Gloria J. (1981). Reciprocity and the coping strategies of older people: Cultural dimensions of network building. The Gerontologist, 21(6), 600-609.

With the use of interviews and participant observation, fifty older people in the urban south were observed with regard to their "helping out" behavior. The paper describes the rules directing the exchange of supports, variations in the interpretations of these rules, and the great personal significance reciprocity has for preserving self-esteem.

Rural

377.   Andrew, Tamara Leigh. (1989). <u>Rural and urban differences in the provision of services to the elderly: An evaluation of a program</u>. Unpublished master's thesis, University of Missouri, Columbia.

An evaluation methodology was used to look at the success of the implementation and maintenance of a model to provide services in both urban and rural sections of a nineteen county area of Missouri. The purpose of the model was to link individual homebound elderly with volunteers, thus combining or complementing community service resources with formal local volunteer organizations. Few significant differences were found, but it is suggested that the model was not successful in the middle range of the urban-rural continuum with resistance to "bureaucratic standards" limiting the success of the model in rural areas.

378.   Goughler, Donald, Young, Christine, & Larson, Pamela. (1984). Organizing volunteer support for the rural elderly. <u>Aging</u>, <u>345</u>, 9-13.

In order to expand resources for older residents of Fayette County, Pennsylvania, the Area Agency on Aging recruited older volunteers from many local existing organizations--serving 442 older residents in the first three years of the project. This article details how the project was structured in this rural setting and how service systems were coordinated.

379.   Halpert, Burton P. (1988). See entry number 208.

380.   Halpert, Burton P., & Sharp, Tessa S. (1989). See entry number 209.

381.   Havir, Linda. (1989, November). <u>Senior centers in rural communities: Potentials for serving</u>. Paper presented at the 42nd annual meeting of the Midwest Sociological Society, Minneapolis, Minnesota.

As part of a study of three senior centers in rural Minnesota, the author looks at the role of the local elderly in the service delivery system. Regarding these roles, questions were asked about the number of volunteers and the types of volunteer activities carried out.

382.   Kay, Bonnie. (1984). See entry number 106.

383.   Mills, Ann K. (1990). See entry number 321.

384.   Patterson, Shirley L., & Brennan, Eileen M. (1983, Summer).
         Matching helping roles with the characteristics of older natural helpers.
         Journal of Gerontological Social Work, 5(4), 55-66.

         The helping approaches of 150 helpers in a rural Kansas community
         (62 paid and 108 natural helpers) were used to study the process of
         matching roles to the capacities, characteristics and values of older
         people.   Older helpers had different values and employed different
         techniques than did their younger counterparts, although each encoun-
         tered similar problems.

385.   Patterson, Shirley L. (1987). Older rural natural helpers: Gender and
         site differences in the helping process. The Gerontologist, 27, 639-
         644.

         This article discusses the results of an investigation of characteristics
         and helping patterns among 45 Midwest and 46 New England, older,
         rural, natural helpers.   While revealing few regional differences,
         findings indicate gender differences with respect to: helper motivation,
         help initiation, helping style, and perceived outcome.   The author
         advises practitioners to support natural helping activities and stresses
         the need for investigations of caregiving by non-family members.

386.   Reynolds, Nancy H. (1988, Spring). Older volunteer leaders in a rural
         community (Marion County, Kansas). The Emporia State Research
         Studies, 36(4).

         This was a study of leadership roles of ten males and ten females who
         were members of a county council on aging situated in rural Kansas.
         The study focused on the paths to volunteering with individual
         examples from the case studies used as illustrations.

387.   Wallin, Theodore, & Kidder, Alice. (1986, August). Financing and
         sustaining mobility programs in rural areas. Washington, DC: U.S.
         Department of Transportation.

         This excellent manual offers a description of volunteer transportation
         systems and discusses: how to determine need, the design and start up
         of programs, and how to sustain such a program. Useful information
         concerning sources of funding and volunteers are provided with several
         profiles of case studies presented.

388.   Young, Christine L., Goughler, Donald H., & Larson, Pamela J. (1986). Organizational volunteers for the rural frail elderly: Outreach, case finding and service delivery. The Gerontologist, 26(4), 342-344.

This is an excellent article describing how community based organizations can be used as focal points of volunteer services for the homebound frail elderly in rural areas. A Model Demonstration Project, conducted in a rural Appalachian county, is outlined in this article, highlighting the importance of volunteer services for both outreach and case finding activities.

Law Enforcement/Crime Victims

389.   American Association of Retired Persons. (1988). Law enforcement
        and older persons (rev. ed.). Washington DC: Author.

        The revised 1988 edition has been updated due to the demand from law
        enforcement professionals who used the 1980 curriculum in order to
        understand and deal more effectively with older persons. This program
        has a module (module four) which provides the framework for the
        planning, implementation, and maintenance of programs involving older
        people in criminal justice support roles--the police, courts and related
        community services. This module focuses on: 1) starting a local
        volunteer program, 2) implementing the program, 3) recruiting and
        placing volunteers and 4) the support and training given.

390.   Coleman, Phillip V. (1989). A study of the feasibility of using retired
        peace officers as volunteers in law enforcement. (Doctoral dissertation,
        Golden Gate University, 1988.) Dissertation Abstracts International,
        50, 540A.

        A survey of three California associations of retired peace officers
        showed that half the respondents supported the idea of using retired
        peace officers as volunteers. Specific tasks were identified as well as
        possible obstacles that might have to be overcome. A transition
        management plan is presented to maximize the success of a retired
        peace officer volunteer program.

391.   Grandparents go to jail. (1984, June-July). See entry number 258.

392.   Senior volunteers to aid crime victims. (1981, Jan-Feb). Aging, 315-
        316, 46-48.

        The federally sponsored Criminal Justice and the Elderly (CJE)
        program--a program in which senior volunteers are used to help
        persons who have been robbed or criminally attacked--is reviewed in
        this article.

393.   Sklar, Ellen, & Carlson, Cathy M. (1987). See entry number 267.

Author Index

Subject Index

Numbers are citation entry numbers, not page numbers.

About the Compilers

C. NEIL BULL is Interim Associate Dean of the College of Arts and Sciences at the University of Missouri at Kansas City. An Associate Professor of sociology there, as well as a Principal Investigator at the National Resource Center for Rural Elderly, he has published widely in journals such as *Society and Culture* and the *Journal of Leisure Research.*

NANCY D. LEVINE is Research Assistant at the National Resource Center for Rural Elderly at the University of Missouri at Kansas City.

www.ingramcontent.com/pod-product-compliance
Lightning Source LLC
Chambersburg PA
CBHW050229270326
41914CB00003BA/638